MW00470294

ADVANCE PRAISE

"*To me, The Great Engagement by Tom Willis and Brad Zimmerman is all about servant leadership in action. The leadership aspect of servant leadership is about aspiration: what is your vision for yourself and your people? Once that's clear, you move to the servant aspect of servant leadership, which is about empowering your people: giving them the capacity to use their talents to make a difference. Reading this book will help you make a difference in the lives of the people you live with, work with, and care about!*"

—KEN BLANCHARD,
COAUTHOR OF *THE NEW ONE MINUTE MANAGER*® AND
SIMPLE TRUTHS OF LEADERSHIP, AMAZON HALL OF FAME
TOP 25 BESTSELLING AUTHOR WITH MORE THAN 28
MILLION BOOKS SOLD IN FORTY-SEVEN LANGUAGES

"*A must read for any CEO serious about culture.*"

—JOSH LINKNER,
NEW YORK TIMES BESTSELLING AUTHOR

"Excellent book by genuine people."

—GINO WICKMAN,
AUTHOR OF *TRACTION* AND *THE EOS LIFE*

"The Great Engagement is a must-read for leaders who want to retain talent, increase employee satisfaction, accelerate results, and transform their organization through servant leadership. This book provides a clear illustration of how a transformative CEO leads with a servant's heart, empowering their employees to achieve greatness. This inspiring and practical guide offers valuable insights into creating a workplace culture that fosters collaboration, innovation, and value for everyone."

—MICHAEL HULL,
PRESIDENT AND CEO OF MAKE-A-WISH® MICHIGAN

"This is a practical guide for any CEO who wants to create an outstanding culture!"

—KATIE SMITH SLOAN,
PRESIDENT AND CEO OF LeadingAge

"Tom and Brad are authentic servant leaders. They masterfully 'hold the space' for conversations, and I always leave provoked, inspired, thoughtful, and with tools to make me a better leader and CEO."

—DAN VARNER,
PRESIDENT AND CHIEF EXECUTIVE OFFICER OF
GOODWILL INDUSTRIES, MICHIGAN

"In The Great Engagement, Brad and Tom bring a deep understanding of organizational and CEO development into one place that sets themselves apart from others. They guide CEOs in leading their organization by declaring their own personal purpose that is directly tied to the 'why' their organization exists. Leading with personal purpose opens the door for everyone in the organization to examine their own purpose and evaluate

whether their why is aligned to the work of the organization. This practice leads to personal and organizational engagement. When everyone is engaged, this is when transformation is able to occur, not only for the organization but for the individual employees. As a CEO this has been the foundational approach I've taken with my executive and leadership team to transform our agency to have results we work hard to achieve."

—Shauna Reitmeier,
CEO of Alluma, board member of the National
Council for Mental Wellbeing

"I've had the privilege of being in a coaching relationship with the authors for more than two decades. This engagement has been the single most impactful influence on my leadership growth, with benefits in my home life as well. More importantly, their work with our organization has been foundational in enabling us to achieve enormous growth and innovation. In this book, Tom and Brad dive directly into the fundamental challenge and opportunity of our time. Tapping into their many decades of study and work with organizations across the country, they lay out a framework for rethinking how to build a culture that harnesses both the passion and capabilities of our teams."

—David Guth,
CEO of Centerstone

"I have tremendous respect for the character and integrity Brad and Tom demonstrate daily. I have long observed the love, care, and concern they have for others. They serve through their efforts to help leaders live their purpose and generate learning environments. I am excited Tom and Brad have decided to put their considerable knowledge into these pages. The methods they share will help you achieve your greatest potential as a leader and give the gift of great leadership to others."

—Kevin Schnieders,
Chief Servant Leader and CEO of EDSI

"Partnering with Tom and Brad exceeded my expectations… The work we did enabled us to grow tenfold over the last five years, and we now have a significantly better team as a result."

—RASHOD JOHNSON,
CEO OF ARDMORE RODERICK

"A practical and effective guide for leadership in the twenty-first century."

—CHAD NEWTON,
CEO OF DETROIT METROPOLITAN AIRPORT (DTW), RANKED BY
J.D. POWER AS #1 IN CUSTOMER SATISFACTION FOR MEGA AIRPORTS

"The guidance Brad and Tom provide in this book has been invaluable to my executive leadership team and me on our journey to transform ourselves and our organization."

—SUSAN HARDING,
PHD, CEO OF OLHSA

"Brad and Tom's contribution to the post-COVID world of leadership is both timely and prescient. The concepts they offer and their ability to convey complex concepts with simplicity and elegance have the power to transform the individual, the team, and entire organizations. I've personally experienced the transformative power of their work and its impact on my organization."

—DAVE GEHM,
CEO OF WELLSPRING LUTHERAN SERVICES

"I am amazed at how this book provides an advanced understanding of how to replace resignation with engagement…producing better results."

—LENORA HARDY-FOSTER,
PRESIDENT AND CEO OF JUDSON CENTER

"Though I've only known Tom and Brad for a few years, their guidance, mentorship, and friendship have had a profound impact on me and my growth as a CEO. Recognizing I will always be a work in progress, I am confident in my ability to lead and learn and grow with their support. The Great Engagement is an insightful, pragmatic guide for leadership, and I highly recommend it for anyone who is committed to creating and nurturing an inspired and empowered organization."

—GENE BOES,
PRESIDENT AND CEO OF NORTHWEST CENTER

"Congratulations on your book and your continued journey to spread the gospel of meaningful engagement and transformation, and for helping us connect the dots to an inspiring, envisioned future."

—GERRY BRISSON,
CEO OF GLEANERS COMMUNITY FOOD BANK

"I love that this book provides practical, executable methods for creating transformational leadership."

—MELANIE BROWN WOOFTER,
PRESIDENT AND CEO OF FBHA

"I've been at this a very long time, and the thing I wanted to avoid was a 'vitamin shot' for our culture. With Tom and Brad, I found a method that sticks and stays. And as much of a believer as I am in the process, my people are that much more. You know it's working when your people are coming to you to say that it's 'profound.'"

—MIKE SIMECK,
SUPERINTENDENT OF DEERFIELD PUBLIC SCHOOLS

"The work we did with Tom and Brad implementing the methods outlined in this book was of huge value to me personally, to our leadership team, and ultimately to the kids we serve!"

—DENNIS MCDAVID,
SUPERINTENDENT EMERITUS OF BERKLEY SCHOOL DISTRICT

"Like capital, employee engagement is a critical resource to a company. Tom and Brad show how a leader can either create or snuff out engagement, so that you can do more of the former."

—EDWIN OLSON,
CEO OF MAY MOBILITY AUTONOMOUS VEHICLES

THE GREAT ENGAGEMENT

THE GREAT

~~RESIGNATION~~

ENGAGEMENT

HOW CEOS CREATE EXCEPTIONAL CULTURES

TOM WILLIS

BRAD ZIMMERMAN

LIONCREST
PUBLISHING

COPYRIGHT © 2024 TOM WILLIS, BRAD ZIMMERMAN
All rights reserved.

THE GREAT ENGAGEMENT
How CEOs Create Exceptional Cultures

FIRST EDITION

ISBN   978-1-5445-3968-3 *Hardcover*
      978-1-5445-3966-9 *Paperback*
      978-1-5445-3967-6 *Ebook*

To Our Fathers in Heaven.

CONTENTS

FROM RESIGNATION TO ENGAGEMENT

AN OVERVIEW

"The mass of men lead lives of quiet desperation. What is called resignation is confirmed desperation."

—HENRY DAVID THOREAU

Employee engagement has come to the forefront in the last decade or so as one of the defining characteristics of great organizations. We all know and appreciate its importance…but what about the opposite?

In all the writing and surveys, the opposite of employee engagement is usually identified as "disengagement." If we take a deeper look at what underlies disengagement, however, we believe that its root more accurately lies in *resignation*.

The dictionary defines *resignation* as "an accepting, unresisting attitude, state, etc.; submission; acquiescence: *to meet one's fate with resignation.*"

This mental state, if allowed to persist, will result in the second definition of *resignation*: "a formal statement or document, stating that one gives up an office or position."

The so-called Great Resignation was caused by years of pent-up resignation. People had a life-altering experience in the COVID-19 pandemic, reassessed their lives, and chose to walk away from jobs about which they felt resignation. So they resigned.

According to Abraham Maslow's famous hierarchy of needs, all human beings strive for self-actualization—the fulfillment of one's potential to make a difference or impact the world. This human impulse is why engagement is so important. When we feel that we are serving a purpose that doesn't impact the world that's important to us, or when we lack the authority or empowerment to make a difference, resignation sets in.

The Great Resignation may be in the rearview mirror, but there is a lesson to be learned from it:

When people feel resigned, if they have a choice, they will resign!

A FORMULA FOR ENGAGEMENT

The two factors we described above, meaningless work and powerlessness, result in resignation. This premise leads us to a simple formula for engagement:

Engagement = Aspiration + Empowerment

People who possess a compelling, aspirational purpose are energized to make an impact. We use the term *purpose* as a general term to include what might be called a vision, mission, goal, and so on. All great leaders aspire to some purpose that compels them to action. This same energy is what fuels exceptional, engaged organizations.

To be empowered is to possess permission to use our talents, creativity, judgment; to utilize the full measure of our capabilities in the service of an aspirational purpose. Some people take this permission themselves, like entrepreneurs, while others need it to be granted, even encouraged to accept it. People who are empowered to unleash their creativity and exercise their judgment, and who are granted the authority to make decisions necessary to accomplish the purpose to which they aspire, experience fulfillment. Empowering people includes encouraging them, appreciating them for their contribution (including commensurate pay), supporting them to be accountable, and coaching them. If either aspiration or empowerment is missing, people will experience resignation.

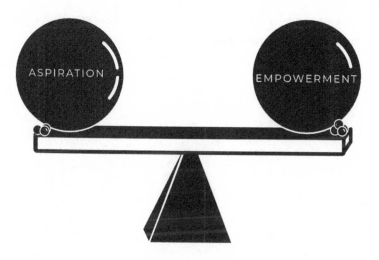

Being on a compelling, aspirational mission is great, but if people don't have the authority and permission to utilize their full capabilities, they are reduced to feeling like robots and are frustrated by their inability to produce the impact they are so excited about.

On the other hand, empowerment without a compelling aspirational purpose results in everyone pursuing their own personal agendas, doing whatever makes them feel comfortable.

In the wake of the pandemic, people in many organizations have emphasized self-care over the aspirational mission, and their organizations' mission fulfillment has suffered. Like many things in life, balance is key. This book will show you, as the CEO, how you can grow your ability to foster greater levels of engagement in your organization by

- energizing your people through aspiration and
- empowering your people.

Ultimately, it will show you how to replace resignation with engagement so your organization can produce better results.

CHAPTER 1

A MILLION-DOLLAR THEFT

"The most perilous risk during times of upheaval isn't the turmoil itself—it's clinging to yesterday's reasoning."

—MAYA ANGELOU

A few decades ago, while we were coaching the leadership team of a finance company, one of the executives confessed on a coaching call that he had stolen $1 million from his employers. This created quite the moral dilemma for us. For now, though, let's concentrate on the real story, which is not how an organization lost money (it got it back, as it happened) but how it discovered its purpose, transformed its people and its culture, and turned their engagement into exceptional and lasting success, moving from being a failing startup to a high-performing powerhouse.

At the time, the firm was struggling to get established. The management team was at war, and the CEO was tearing his hair out. The firm was a startup that catered to small businesses that were too new to get conventional financing, and investors had poured in capital because they could see the growth and profit potential in this niche. It was a great business model, but a couple of years in, the investors were getting frustrated. The business wasn't growing, and their projected ROI hadn't materialized.

The head of sales, and the head of underwriting, who approved loans, had constant knock-down, drag-out arguments: "You keep turning down all the great customers I bring in." "Well, you keep bringing in customers with no creditworthiness." The CEO, who had been in the business for thirty years, told them, "Cut this s*#t out" and walked out of the room.

That didn't help the two of them get along any better.

The rest of the management team kept their heads down to the point of disengaging from the team. Everyone was pretty frustrated and resigned about their ability to change the dynamic and their potential for success. Eventually, the CEO reached out and engaged us to run a program we call the Transformational Leadership Experience for his seven-member executive team, consisting of an intensive 2½ day workshop followed by five months of executive coaching and customized support.

As part of the workshop, we engaged them in individual exercises and a group discussion focused on these questions: *What was their personal purpose in life? What made them come to work every day?* They said it was making money. We told them that wasn't a purpose and to try again. This time, they said it was providing a return on investment to their investors. Money, again. And hogwash, again. We explained that money is a scoreboard, and an important one, that tells you whether or not you're being successful at your purpose; but money is never a purpose.

The hard-nosed executives didn't like that, but we kept encouraging them to think less like capitalists, focused purely on numbers and money, and more like the whole human beings they each brought with them to the office every day. We had them talk about their personal core values, not just at work but as spouses, parents, friends, church-goers, members of the community. They were instinctively resistant to what they saw as so much nonsense. They wanted to keep themselves and their work separate. The conversation got heated.

We kept asking questions to get them to think about their personal motivations. "What is your personal purpose in life?" "What's the legacy you want to leave?" "What do you want your eulogy to say?"

The breakthrough came after lunch on the second day. Collectively they realized that, despite what they'd always assumed in their previous finance jobs, their purpose was not about making money at all.

Their purpose was to make the small businesses they worked with financially viable, to significantly increase these businesses' credit ratings, and to help their customers grow to new levels of success. Not only would that give client organizations more financial viability. It would also bring more economic vitality to the region and create jobs—and they would become known as the organization that gives a leg up to small businesses.

They found a new sense of purpose—one to engage in that replaced their resignation with an aspirational purpose—and it was an epiphany for them all. It was something everyone in the room could aspire to.

For the next several months, they worked on evoking this same aspiration from every employee, generating a compelling commitment to this aspirational purpose from each employee. They discussed their purpose in every meeting and used it to guide their decisions. They posted their personal purposes throughout the office as reminders. The interpersonal conflicts were lessened now that they all committed to the same purpose and realized they had to work together to achieve it.

The organizations they helped were so grateful they provided lots of referrals, so their client acquisition process became much easier and its reputation grew. Within a few years, they were making exceptional returns for their investors and great money for themselves, and they had more satisfied customers than they had ever dreamed.

There was an unexpected bonus, too. Soon after the workshop, Brad took a call from one of the attendees who confessed that he had stolen a million bucks from the firm. He said, "I don't even know why I'm telling you this." Brad responded, "I think you told me this because you can't live with yourself anymore."

It was true. Once he realized that his own personal purpose was to help others, it was clear he had to confess. Brad spent a couple of weeks talking him into also telling his CEO. He did, and he repaid the money. He was fired—of course!—but the CEO forgave him, and did not press charges.

He recognized the power of replacing his unconscious greed with a conscious decision to serve others. This clarity of purpose transformed him, and six months later, he asked Brad to work with his new team at his next place of employment.

OUR UNCONSCIOUS PURPOSE

Few companies suffer a million-dollar theft—but many don't reach their full potential. Their teams are being held back, and CEOs can't understand why. That's frustrating, because CEOs are great at coming up with solutions to problems—but not when they can't identify what the problem is.

In the wake of the Great Resignation, it's more critical than ever that your team is engaged in what they do. If they aren't, the consequence is resignation, which leads to watching good people leave for reasons you don't fully understand. Productivity and profitability suffer.

Here are a few figures to back up our point:

- **66 percent:** the proportion of US workers who feel disengaged, according to a Gallup report
- **74 percent:** the proportion of those workers who are either actively looking for new work or are open to new opportunities
- **550 million:** the number of days off a year that the stress associated with not being fully engaged at work costs the US economy, according to the American Psychological Association
- **$500 billion:** the cost to the economy of those days off

At times, we can all become resigned. It happens *unconsciously* and is part of how the unconscious mind stores what we have learned. It's human nature. Whether you recognize it or not, you are resigned about many things also.

UNCONSCIOUS, NOT ASLEEP

We use the word *unconscious*, not to refer to someone who is asleep, or lying on the ground knocked out, but to the workings of our minds that we are not aware of because they do not involve conscious thought. That does not only include autonomic functions such as the regulation of our heart rate, but also the assumptions we make (like unconscious bias), many of our motivations (like someone who is driven to succeed), and competencies (like ability to write, or type). All of these things occur without conscious thought.

The first step to getting beyond that resignation is to recognize it. How resigned are you about your ability to increase employee engagement?

In the 1960s, President Eisenhower was given a white tiger named Mohini. Eisenhower sent the tiger to the Washington Zoo, where it paced restlessly in a tiny cage. After some years, a sponsor paid to build Mohini a large pen full of grass and trees. When Mohini was put into her new home, however, she didn't explore. Instead, she went into the farthest corner of the enclosure, and spent the rest of her life pacing in an area the size of her former cage. Even an animal as ferocious as a tiger can become resigned.

Resignation is like a box that limits what we do. It's learned behavior, based on past experience. We unconsciously assume that we have to keep within its limits.

To get out of the box, we have to first know that we're in a box.

Humans become trapped by past assumptions that no longer apply to our lives. The bars never existed or have been taken away—and we don't notice. It's the role of organizational leaders to show people that what they think are their limits are not real. When exceptional leaders do this, their team members gain access to more of their potential, become conscious of their goals, more engaged to reach them, and more fulfilled.

CEOs often try to improve engagement. Perhaps they call in team-building consultants who take their teams on rope-climbing courses to build trust, or they pass around a talking stick as they commit to getting along better with their colleagues. Those approaches might make things better for a while, *but their effects don't last.* They can even make things worse when people realize that how others behave during team-building exercises makes no difference at all to how they behave at work.

Most interventions don't address the real problem, because it's impossible to solve a problem people don't know exists.

Thought leaders talk a lot about disengagement, but many only address its symptoms, not its cause. Most engagement surveys and profiles focus on issues: whether you've been acknowledged recently, whether you have a best friend at work, what you think of your manager. These are good things, but they are symptoms of engagement or disengagement, not root causes. This obscures the causes of engagement. *Engagement derives from each person being committed to the purpose of the organization and seeing it as **their own aspiration**.* Engagement means engagement in the mission, and it's seldom talked about. There are many books that address purpose, but most focus on the signs of purpose and not about how to introduce purpose into people's lives.

In the absence of such an engaging purpose, human beings default to their unconscious purpose. This unconscious purpose is almost always fear based because it supports our instinct for self-survival. In modern society, that equates to staying in our comfort zone. The problem that holds *your* organization back lies in the unconscious mind of your team (which includes you).

Each of us has a purpose that motivates our behavior without us being aware of it. This unconscious purpose has served us well in the past, so it becomes our comfort zone.

Staying in our comfort zone is a natural reaction. It's part of being human. Our ancestors developed it as a behavior to reduce risk in a world that was full of real dangers beyond their caves or shelters. It's based on a single emotion: fear.

Perhaps the word *fear* seems a little strong to you. You may prefer to think of it as just feeling a little "uncomfortable." It's the same thing, but in our society, we are "uncomfortable" admitting our fears. Part of the goal of this book is to convince you that it's fine to use the word *fear* without any baggage.

On an unconscious level, humans are still largely driven by fear, only today most of those fears are no longer real; they're imaginary. These fears are not about life-threatening situations; they're about the imagined fear of failure, the imagined fear that people won't like us or that we won't fit in. They're not about physical, existential threats; they're about what our minds tell us might go wrong.

THINGS I
WORRY ABOUT

THINGS THAT
CAN HAPPEN

THINGS THAT
DO HAPPEN

As Mark Twain once observed, "I've had a lot of worries in my life, most of which never happened."

THE ENEMY WITHIN

Fear comes from a small region of the brain called the amygdala. The amygdala is commonly thought to form the core of a neural system for processing fearful and threatening stimuli. It triggers flight, fight, or freeze. The latest brain research calls it a novelty detector, scanning the world for signs of anything new or unexpected. Given that this fear center is triggered by anything new, is it any wonder why humans resist change? In addition, the amygdala is what causes us to react to an email or text message as if it were life threatening when in fact it's simply Sally from accounting asking us to change the way we fill in our expense forms. It's what makes us react to a comment from a coworker like they're attacking us with a knife. It's the unconscious that causes so many of our problems.

Brain scans suggest that the amygdala reacts with the same instinctual fear to the question "Are you open to some feedback?" as it does to hearing unknown footsteps following us in the dark. With our amygdala on guard with this intensity, is it any wonder that many managers avoid coaching their people?

The amygdala ensures that anything "new" in our lives results in us retreating to our comfort zones. We automatically and unconsciously behave in the ways we've found successful in the past for staying comfortable...or avoiding fear.

We call this kind of reaction to our fears *the fur-lined rut*. Fur lined, because it feels like a comfortable place to be—and rut, because it's a course from which it's very difficult to change.

Perhaps this is true for you. Many CEOs suffer from imposter syndrome: a fear that they don't belong in the position or that they don't know what they are doing. Some love their team so much that they are afraid to make the changes they know they need to make. Others are fearful they won't be innovative enough to lead the organization into an uncertain future. And still others are fearful that they won't have all the answers.

We know that being the CEO can be a very lonely job. What about you—what keeps you up at night?

In the example of the fractious leadership team of the finance company, the head of underwriting was a meticulous thinker, which qualified him well for assessing risks on a loan. But he was such a perfectionist that he criticized the salespeople for bringing in poor credit risks—and that was exactly the sort of client they were seeking. On the other hand, the head of sales was very social and inclusive, and didn't hear the underwriter's criticism as a helpful perspective on the prospects he found. He took it as an insult.

Both leaders were being driven by an unconscious purpose: their fear of failure. They both wanted to "make their numbers" and demonstrate they could do the job. This unconscious purpose of avoiding failure resulted in each of them myopically pursuing their own targets without consideration for the other's role. It became a personal battle: "You're a pain in the a** and nobody is good enough for you." And "you just want to try to make yourself look good, and you're going to sink this bank in the process."

They lacked a conscious purpose, a higher purpose than making themselves look good.

EXCEPTIONAL CULTURE

What does a conscious purpose have to do with creating an exceptional culture?

Culture is made up of the socially constructed beliefs, behaviors, and ground rules shared within any group.

None of us makes a conscious decision to act in a particular way while we're heading into the office. The way we behave as a group is the sum of the behaviors we bring along as individuals. So to create an exceptional culture, we have to help the individuals within that culture change their beliefs, behaviors, and self-imposed limitations.

Exceptional leaders understand this and consider every day as a chance to intentionally shape their culture.

No attempt to change company culture can work if it doesn't address the unconscious fears that shape it. Real change comes from showing people that we don't need to be limited by our unconscious motivations. And that requires replacing our unconscious purpose with a conscious commitment to a higher purpose. It is transformational.

It's transformational because it is a fundamental change to the whole structure of how people work. It's not tweaking or improving how to run a meeting. It's not about taking trust falls. It's not about incremental change. Transformation helps people see themselves and their jobs completely differently than they did a few weeks beforehand...or even a few moments ago...

Ongoing personal transformation involves CEOs and their teams aligning their behavior with a higher purpose rather than with their comfort zone. They learn a new frame of reference based on aspirational commitment. Their transformation leads to more inspiration, engagement in purpose, inclusivity, psychological safety, and accountability, resulting in personal growth with greater levels of impact and value on those they serve. Together, this creates a transformational culture that drives engagement.

BILLIONS OF DOLLARS ARE SPENT
EVERY YEAR ON CULTURE CHANGE
EFFORTS, AND MOST OF THAT
MONEY IS WASTED. SO WHAT MAKES
CULTURE SO DIFFICULT TO CHANGE?

CULTURE IS MOSTLY UNCONSCIOUS.

We always have a choice: our Comfort, or our Higher Purpose.

This type of transformation has instant, wide-ranging benefits:

- It replaces chronic resignation (the source of burnout) with engagement, which is energizing.
- It generates *personal commitment* to aspirational missions or visions.
- It improves relationships and, therefore, communication.
- It increases personal responsibility, accountability, integrity, creativity, inclusion, empowerment, and trust.
- It drives personal growth by raising self-awareness that allows people to identify counterproductive behaviors and develop new behaviors.
- It allows team members to support each other in moving beyond their comfort zones and operate in the learning zone.
- It brings humanity and humility to our organizations.

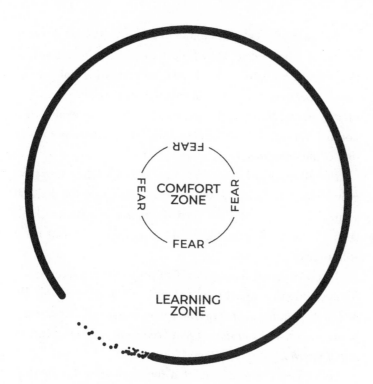

BACK TO THE FINANCE COMPANY

Let's go back to the struggling startup. The boss was a first-time CEO with a vision of a firm in a new segment with a new business model. He was struggling to build a culture that supported that business model. But his Default Success Strategy was to fall back on the controlling, punitive behavior that had worked in his previous job. That wasn't working.

Once we got the CEO and his leadership team to understand how their unconscious purposes were preventing them from realizing their higher purpose—which was to help small organizations achieve financial stability—things started to change as they began to become more conscious of their actions.

The head of sales, who wanted to do business with everyone, realized that he needed to be a little more selective in terms of the prospects he brought in. The head of underwriting realized that he was operating out of his fear that the bank would lose money on a loan, and that his job was actually to take reasonable risks, not to avoid risk. The two of them came to a middle point where they could work together.

That all happened twenty-five years ago. Since then, they have grown many times in size and become a player on the national scene. The $1-million theft turned out not to have any long-lasting impact—but the legacy of transformational leadership still survives.

This may sound simple: just help people be more conscious. It's not quite that straightforward. *As we will see, it requires the conscious application of **transformational leadership**, **empowering management**, and **transformational coaching**—the most important of which is **transformational leadership**.*

Let's take a closer look at what transformational leadership is...and how you can use it to foster engagement.

WHAT IS TRANSFORMATIONAL LEADERSHIP?

"We hold these truths to be self-evident: that all men are created equal; that they are endowed by their Creator with certain unalienable rights; that among these are life, liberty, and the pursuit of happiness."

—THOMAS JEFFERSON

An old Cherokee parable tells us about a grandfather who was teaching his grandson about life. "A fight is going on inside me," he said to the boy. "It is a terrible fight between two wolves. One is evil: he is fear, anger, envy, sorrow, regret, greed, arrogance, self-pity, guilt, resentment, inferiority, lies, false pride, superiority, and ego. The other is good: he is joy, peace, love, hope, serenity, humility, kindness, benevolence, empathy, generosity, truth, compassion, and faith. This same fight is going on inside you—and inside every other person, too."

The grandson thought about it for a minute and then asked, "Which wolf will win?"

His grandfather simply replied, "The one you feed."

POWER OF TRANSFORMATION

Transformational leadership is about moving people from resignation to engagement. The word *transformational* is used so much in today's society that it has lost all meaning. For example, trying a new breakfast cereal or changing your hairstyle gets tagged as "transformational"!

If we could use a different word, we would—but *transformational* is the only word that means what we want to say: a change in the fundamental character of a person or a culture.

There are examples all around us, like the young couple who, upon finding that they are pregnant with their first child, give up their reckless, partying lifestyle and start eating sensibly, buy a home, and start to make decisions based on their child's welfare. Or the widow who begins joining clubs and throwing herself into community activities so that her family feels less responsible for helping to occupy her time.

Every leader transforms themselves continually and has done so many times in the past. Just think of what you were like in your twenties and how you have grown since then. Think of how you had to change the first time you sat in a chair behind a desk and thought, *I'm in charge.* Think of the fundamental changes in character you've gone through.

The method shared in this book allows you to accelerate that transformation dramatically. Instead of taking decades, it takes months.

Foundational to this method is the concept of high-impact learning. It combines learning a concept with experiencing that concept in the real world. Together, that solidifies understanding by growing the neural connections in our brains—creating a lasting, meaningful impact and sustainable growth.

A CONSCIOUS RESPONSE

The essence of transformational leadership is replacing an unconscious emotional reaction to a situation with a more thoughtful and conscious response. This distinction is so simple, yet so challenging to live—*am I reacting emotionally or am I responding thoughtfully?*

Imagine that you find yourself in a heated discussion with someone who means a lot to you, perhaps your spouse, partner, a parent or child. It's easy to feel defensive or under attack in difficult conversations like that, and you feel that you need to lash out to defend yourself.

So you find yourself about to say something that you know won't help the relationship; in fact, it will press a button and escalate matters, but instead, you make a different choice. You think, *I could "win" this argument if I make this point or make them feel dumb…but this person means more to me than driving my point home or proving I'm right. I'm more committed to this relationship than I am to winning this argument.* That's how simple it is to take an extra moment to come up with a more thoughtful, measured response. **But being simple does not make it easy.** Being aware enough to catch the fear and the anger that arises from it is hard work.

This is the essence of transformation. When we stop reacting emotionally, we respond thoughtfully. It's simple. It's elegant. It's productive.

But it's not easy, as we've all learned from making that more instinctive choice that escalated matters and turned a heated discussion into a fight, someone getting grounded, or even a night on the couch. There are times when it seems that every urge in our bodies is telling us to press the button and take the nuclear option. It's not easy to resist what seems natural. That's why transformational leadership is an acquired skill; it's a learned behavior that requires training and practice. And before we master transformational leadership, we must embrace transformation itself.

Make no mistake, though: transformation is possible. When the stakes are important enough, people take heroic steps. We've seen transformations that seem almost miraculous. Anyone can overcome their emotional knee-jerk reaction once they embrace their higher purpose. Consider a young parent who is shy and quiet, and terrified of public speaking. But their child is having a rough time at school because of a new policy, and the parent feels passionately that the policy must be reversed. Despite their fear, the parent stands up in front of hundreds of people at a crowded PTA meeting to express this view. The love of their child overrides their fear of speaking out. They are more committed to their child's success than their own comfort.

TRANSFORMATIONAL LEADERS

Transformational leadership isn't a new fad. It has existed throughout history. It's at the heart of historically impactful groups such as the Founding Fathers; the blacksmiths, military leaders, rebels, politicians, writers, and farmers who changed the world; or the "Greatest Generation" of World War II, who experienced personal transformation en masse and committed to themselves to defeating Nazism.

Many of the world's major religions had transformational leaders, including Jesus, Muhammad, Moses, Buddha, and the Gurus of Sikhism. In many ways, Jesus can be seen as the greatest transformational leader of all. He came along and changed how people thought about everything. No more eye for an eye, as society had embraced for centuries. In fact, Jesus suggested to do the opposite: turn the other cheek. Imagine what a radical, transformational message this was. *"What are you talking about, turn the other cheek? We've practiced our eye-for-an-eye law forever! You expect us to do the exact opposite?"* And Jesus did that in every single area of life. His commandment, "Thou shalt love thy neighbor as thyself" (Matthew 22:39), flipped the world upside down, and "the Golden Rule" has been the inspiration for transformation for millions over the millennia.

The American Founding Fathers were a collection of farmers and shopkeepers, many with little education, when they were thrust into a leadership role by an unignorable sense of injustice. The treatment of colonial Americans by their British governors left them with no choice but to lead a campaign for fair treatment that escalated into a revolution and the creation of the Republic. They declared their higher purpose when they proposed that all men are created equal and have inalienable rights, despite their knowledge that their own individual attitudes to other people were far from perfect. Such was the power of that purpose that it converted the rabble—and it *was* a rabble, full of flawed, unlikely leaders—into a generation that led the Revolution, achieved independence, and created a whole new form of government based on the startling new concept of individual rights. They framed the Constitution and transformed the political landscape of North America, and their legacy has shaped the world for the last 250 years.

There are endless examples of transformational leadership. How about the Suffragists, ordinary women who risked ridicule, violence, and punishment in their struggle around the turn of the twentieth century to win the vote for women? How about the generation of young men who enlisted after Pearl Harbor on

December 7, 1941, to fight to save democracy, or the civilians at home, like "Rosie the Riveter," who changed their lives overnight to support the war effort? How about the college dropouts who learned coding in their parents' garages in the 1970s to lead the world into the digital age? These are all examples of people choosing a noble purpose over their own personal comfort.

There's plenty of evidence that transformational leadership works. It's not just some theoretical New Age theory. It's grounded in reality—and it has practical results. It teaches pragmatic lessons to improve our lives inside and outside the workplace.

PURPOSE AND EFFECT

We define transformational leadership as this: *Generating a vision for the future that people adopt as their future. This future becomes their aspiration. Such a vision changes people's focus from an unconscious, fear-based purpose of self-protection to a consciously generated love-based purpose of contributing to the growth or benefit of others.* As a leader, you inspire team members to move beyond behaving in ways driven merely by their habitual, automatic behaviors. You encourage them to shift from a defensive, fear-based response to one driven by a commitment to their own higher purpose.

To become a transformational leader requires you first to be aware of your own higher purpose and to consciously commit to a purpose that's bigger than yourself.

This requires effort, from yourself and also from the individuals with whom you work. The effect transformational leadership has on both individuals and organizations is staggering. The usual ego-based factors that motivate people in the workplace create division and silos. Motivation by our best selves, in contrast, is a unifying force that allows everyone to work together to achieve more.

GENERATING A VISION FOR
THE FUTURE THAT PEOPLE
ADOPT AS THEIR FUTURE.

The best organizations have cultures that foster daily transformation among their people. None of us gets "transformed" once and considers the work done—this is never-ending work. That's why we refer to it not as a transformation but as *transformational.* "Transformational" implies a series of conscious decisions: becoming aware when emotions are motivating your actions, assessing if that's the most effective response, and choosing what action to take.

It is a moment-by-moment process—and it won't happen overnight. Creating an exceptional culture will take a conscious and intentional commitment on your part. There are no quick tips or tricks. The key is to start and keep going. After all, Babe Ruth struck out 1,330 times. Picasso is renowned for 100 or so masterpieces he created, but less so for the close to 50,000 more obscure works he produced. Benjamin Franklin didn't invent bifocal eyeglasses until he was seventy-nine; Frank Lloyd Wright was ninety-one when he completed the Guggenheim Museum; and Ichijiro Araya was one hundred years old when he climbed Mount Fuji. The trick is never to give up and never to stop.

WHAT GREAT RESIGNATION?

There is a very pragmatic reason for today's CEOs to embrace transformational leadership: the ongoing shortage of people in the workforce that followed the Great Resignation. Millions of people have turned their backs on their jobs, causing a global crisis.

It doesn't have to be like that. The answer to the Great Resignation is a Great Engagement. More than ever, a CEO needs the ability to develop their team members not simply to help them acquire the skills they need to be effective, but also to help them learn behaviors that will make their work far more fulfilling by linking it to a higher purpose beyond themselves.

You'll know when you have achieved that when you see improved team-member retention and customer satisfaction, and a healthier bottom line.

Such a strategy requires not just conventional leadership, but transformational leadership. Conventional leadership relies on policies, procedures, discipline: the *how* to do things. Transformational leadership relies on awareness, potential, and inspiration: that's the *why that drives who people are being*.

Imagine a coach with two athletes learning to run track. With one athlete, the coach sticks to technicalities. The coach shows them how to start, how to kick, how to lengthen their stride, how to dip toward the tape. The athlete might become a really good runner—but if they're not *committed* to running track, not *passionate* about running track, the chances are that they won't keep going when it gets difficult. It's a lot of work, after all, and it takes them way outside their comfort zone for a reward they don't really appreciate.

With the other athlete, the coach doesn't start with the technicalities of track. The coach starts with stories of great athletes from the past, or stories of their own past performances, or famous meets they attended. They describe the elation of running as fast as you can and feeling your own strength. They share the satisfaction of pulling on their running spikes in the early dawn as their breath mists in the air. They *inspire* the athlete to want to run track. Now the athlete has the commitment and the passion to keep showing up and doing the work. Teaching them the technicalities is an important but secondary consideration.

Transformational leadership inspires rather than instructs. We often joke that we're not about training. Training is for puppies. **Training won't transform cultures, leaders, and team members— but you *can* inspire them to commit to a higher purpose that motivates new behaviors.**

THE ANSWER TO THE
GREAT RESIGNATION IS A
GREAT ENGAGEMENT.

When the great Renaissance artist Michelangelo looked at a block of marble, he didn't just see a piece of stone—he could see David hidden inside it. He chipped away at the marble to free the figure he already knew was inside the stone. In the same way, as a transformational leader, you have the power to look at your team members and **not only see the potential inside them, but also to help them unlock it.**

Transformational leadership engages people in a way that allows them to unlock behaviors and whole new ways of being. And a team of people growing and improving in this way is the antidote to the emotions that can get in the way of unlocking potential.

GO TALK TO THEM

Our amygdala remains as sensitive as ever to what it perceives as threats, and it's always ready to trigger a fear response. The fears that have kept humanity alive for millennia are now more likely to be triggered by Erika from Accounting not copying us on an email; or Fred not asking our opinion in a meeting. We might imagine he doesn't respect us, but it's rare that incidents like that are motivated by a malign purpose that would justify a fearful response. More often, they are mere oversights or accidents that can be resolved with a simple conversation. In fact, many of our coaching calls around perceived communication breakdowns and personality clashes end with a version of the same advice: "Go talk to them."

We often joke that one day we'll write a book called *Go Talk to Them*. Inside, it will say, "Go talk to them. The End."

But we knew we had to write *The Great Engagement* first.

A CLIENT'S JOURNEY

One of our clients grew up in the inner city. Early on, Isaiah was fortunate to have a mentor who persuaded him he could accomplish really great things no matter what society told him. It wasn't so much of an epiphany as a series of small realizations: that he could get a proper education, that he could become an architect or an engineer, and that that would enable him to buy one of those homes on the other side of town that he had only ever seen from the outside. Then he could send his kids to good schools, and in turn they would have a better life.

The key step came when Isaiah's mentor helped him gain admission to a private school where he got an education not just in math and science, which would prepare him for an engineering career, but in the ways successful people operated—by networking, leveraging contacts, learning to communicate effectively.

Starting in his attic by himself, Isaiah launched an architectural firm that would eventually log annual revenue of $80 million a year…and guess what? He wasn't satisfied with that. Having benefited so much from his own personal transformation, he wanted to pay it forward. He wanted to become a transformational leader to help other disadvantaged kids follow in his footsteps.

Isaiah's goal is nothing less than to help transform the perception of Black-owned organizations, and to serve as a model nationwide for young Black people launching their own businesses. This required still more transformation; it's one thing to build a superior widget, and quite another to build a team focused on enabling others to transform—especially when many of those folks come from difficult environments that actively discourage such thinking.

In his mid-forties, Isaiah is so successful that he could retire and never work another day in his life. Instead, he's helping young people nationwide pursue success. He's a man on a mission to transform how young people respect and honor themselves so they can grow up and go into the world with a conviction to serve others and make a difference in the world.

Both Isaiah and the mentor who helped him see his life in a new way are transformational leaders. You can become one, too. All CEOs and leaders can aspire to transformational leadership— so why don't we?

To be completely frank, it's because transformational leadership is difficult. Most leaders are more comfortable managing tasks and processes than inspiring transformation, which involves vulnerability, self-knowledge, and human emotions. It's not comfortable, and sometimes it can be pretty messy. As we've explained, however, we believe that a leader's job is to help people grow—and that if leaders don't help their people grow in the current workforce environment, they'll lose them.

Simply by picking up this book and reading it this far, you've demonstrated the desire to become a transformational leader. Let's take a deeper look and examine the mental model behind transformational leadership.

EMOTIONS: SERVANT OR MASTER?

"He who has overcome his fears will truly be free."

—ARISTOTLE

As a leader, you already know that it takes courage to lead. It takes courage to make difficult or unpopular decisions, to take risks, to deliver bad news.

But what is courage? Some people think it's the absence of fear, but all humans experience fear. Courage is feeling the fear and doing it anyway.

As a leader, you are regularly called upon to put yourself in situations ranging from uncomfortable to downright frightening: *"People aren't going to like this decision." "This could scare away some customers." "If I get this wrong, my board might fire me."*

WE ARE EMOTIONAL BEINGS

There's almost nothing we do that isn't driven by emotion. That's the way we're wired. The origin of the word *emotion* is the same as the origin of the word *motivate*. Emotions set us in motion.

And yet we're unconscious of most of the emotions in our lives. The simple fact that we realize that courage is necessary for leadership illustrates that, no matter how logical or rational we may think we are, fear is almost always present. Otherwise, we wouldn't need courage.

Our emotions can overwhelm our rational thought processes. Our prefrontal cortex, which is our thinking mind, has access to about two linear feet of information; our unconscious mind, which is governed by emotion, has access to about ten soccer fields' worth of information. That's why epiphanies seem to come when we go for a walk or take a shower. Our brain is working away unconsciously with all its hidden information to come up with a sudden idea.

Most workplaces expect people to leave their emotions at home, so we show up as purely professional versions of ourselves. That's like asking us to leave our humanness at home. We think of emotions as bad things, as in a phrase like "Don't bring your emotional baggage to the office." But emotions can be hugely positive. Emotions move us; in fact, the word "emotion" comes from the Latin *movere*, meaning "to move." Emotions can move us to become excited about accomplishing something. They fire people up.

In the 1970s, Elisabeth Kubler-Ross identified two foundational emotions that give rise to all other emotions. They are at the opposite ends of the emotional spectrum.

The first is fear.

Fear is our reaction to a perceived threat, whether that threat is real or imagined. Fear gives rise to anger, frustration, impatience (fight) or to helplessness, guilt, loneliness, and resignation/disengagement (flight or freeze).

The second emotion is the other end of the spectrum: love. This requires some clarification. The English language has but one word ("love") to express many types of love. The love we possess for our children is different from the love we possess for our spouse, which is different from the love we express for our best friend. **The love we are referring to here is the willful, conscious investment of oneself for the growth or benefit of another.** It's what the ancient Greeks referred to as *agape* (pronounced ah-gah-PAY) love.

Agape love gives rise to peace, patience, kindness, goodness, faithfulness, gentleness, gratitude, serenity, interest, joy, self-control, amusement, hope, awe, flow…and engagement.

The Irish playwright George Bernard Shaw once observed:

> This is the true joy in life, the being used for a purpose recognized by yourself as a mighty one; the being a force of nature instead of a feverish, selfish little clod of ailments and grievances complaining that the world will not devote itself to making you happy.

Shaw highlights the fact that people gain true joy by aspiring to a higher purpose that makes a difference for others. Our fears unconsciously move us more toward being only a "little clot of ailments and grievances." But we can replace those unconscious fears with a conscious purpose: a decision to help people find their mission in life and to live consistently with it to make a lasting impact on the world—a decision to bring spirit to the workplace and to people's lives.

SEPARATE MINDSETS

Fear and love set up two separate dispositions, or mindsets, which are both cyclical, self-reinforcing loops.

Fear causes us to focus on ourselves: *"What's best for me?"*

Love is the conscious focus on others—*"How do I serve others?"*—that creates great people and great organizations.

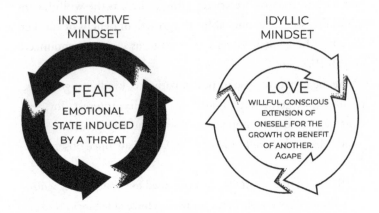

This simple distinction between being focused on *me* (my fears) or focused on *others* (my desire to contribute to them) is transformative. **It determines who we are in the world and what difference we will make:** for our families, our team members, our communities, our customers.

Fear leads to an instinctive mindset and an unconscious vicious cycle, in which fear leads to fear and to more fear, until we end up spinning out of control.

Love leads to an idyllic, conscious mindset. In this virtuous cycle, love leads to love, which leads to more love.

Fear is almost ever-present in everyone. As we've seen, our amygdala is constantly triggered by anything novel or unusual. Very few people wake up and think, *Yeah! I get to make a presen-*

tation to the board today. Most people think, *Oh God, what's going to happen with my presentation today?*

Imagining negative scenarios can be helpful because they prepare us to get "up" for those performances, but they're still the product of fear.

In evolutionary terms, our amygdala, the fear-generator in our brain, is designed to warn us of existential, physical threats from approaching tigers and warring tribes. **In First World society, most of the fears we experience in organizations are imagined:** *What if I fail? What if they don't like me? What if I'm wrong? What if I get fired?*

Questions like these are rooted in fear and can lead anyone, or any team, into a vicious cycle.

THE VICIOUS CYCLE

When we wake up in the morning experiencing fear, the fear can be as simple as "I know I've got more to do today than I can get done." Underlying that feeling is a foundational fear that "I'm not capable or competent enough to do the job." That fear triggers our amygdala into an unconscious purpose of self-survival. In modern society, however, that translates into a purpose such as "I'm going to prove that I'm capable of doing this job and show everyone."

Our fear-based unconscious purpose generally falls into a few categories. We want to prove that we are right, we want to look good in the eyes of others, or we want to prove that we are capable. We don't think about this. It's completely unconscious.

When we are on autopilot, our unconscious purpose is to avoid fear by staying in our comfort zone. We all strive for comfort, which is achieved when we eliminate anything our amygdala sees as a threat. A simple example: we strive to stay warm and dry to be comfortable. These needs are states that we are generally not aware of striving for, such as a need for contact with other people, which might make us more sociable than the next person, or a need to make sure people are comfortable around us. This set of needs comprises our Comfort Zone. As we have said, human behavior is driven largely by our commitment to comfort.

Throughout history people have endeavored to understand and describe the attributes that define the comfort zone for which people strive. The first known attempt was in 2000 BC by Babylonian astrologers, who believed that four elements formed the basis of human behavior: fire, water, earth, and air. In 400 BC the Greek physician Hippocrates argued that differing levels of four bodily fluids; blood, black bile, green bile and phlegm, produced four temperaments: melancholy, sanguine, phlegmatic, and choleric. In 1923 Carl Jung, the father of analytical psychology, described four psychological types: feeler, thinker, intuitor, and sensor. Modern brain science advances the belief that our behavior is driven by four major brain chemicals: dopamine, acetylcholine, GABA, and serotonin.

While there have been many explanations as to the cause of our needs—humors, fluids, astrology, or brain chemicals—the understanding that different proportions of four characteristics in different people make up our comfort zone has been consistent for thousands of years.

We describe these four basic human needs as:

- **Control:** to create a sense of being master of a situation, relationship or circumstance
- **Interaction:** to be "connected" and in relationship with others
- **Stability:** to experience a familiar, unchanging, reliable environment
- **Perfection:** to ensure "correctness" through facts and structure

These needs do not define who we are; they are simply the things that we strive for in order to remain comfortable. Remember, we strive for these things unconsciously. The amount of importance we unconsciously place on each of the four needs defines our comfort zone.

DEFAULT SUCCESS STRATEGY™

That unconscious purpose then leads to a personal behavioral style—what we refer to as a Default Success Strategy™.

When we're young, we design behaviors to help us obtain what we want and file them away in our emotional mind for future access. We develop Default Success Strategies, which are behaviors that become our unconscious, automatic methods for success. We're so accustomed to them that we believe they're hard-wired into our personalities. Our Default Success Strategies are the behaviors we use unconsciously to avoid fear or stay comfortable. As we saw earlier, our unconscious purpose is to remain in our comfort zone.

No one wakes up in the morning and says, "I think I'll be controlling today," or "I think I'll strive for perfection today." We employ these strategies unconsciously, because they are the default setting for our behavior. That leads us to the conclusion that it's "just the way we are." **Our Default Success Strategies are the accumulation of strengths we've learned to employ throughout our lives to achieve success or comfort.** We utilize these strategies by default...automatically. Because we utilize those strategies without being consciously aware we're employing them, we tend to use them even in situations where they don't work. In other words...

Your Default Success Strategies work great...until they don't.

FEAR

UNCONSCIOUS PURPOSE:
SELF-SURVIVAL
STAY IN COMFORT ZONE

PERSONAL
BEHAVIORAL STYLE:
DEFAULT SUCCESS STRATEGY

So if we are someone who tends to take control and we have too much to do today, we go into survival mode. Our Default Success Strategy takes over: "I'm going to take charge, power through, and get everything done, no matter who gets in my way."

Because this whole process is designed to eliminate fear by staying in our comfort zone, it is by definition a "personal agenda." That personal agenda may be something as innocent as "I'm just here for a paycheck" (and wanting a paycheck isn't a bad thing by the way).

Our personal agenda and our Default Success Strategy lead to a general mindset that affects us individually and pervades our culture. Not all of the attributes of this mindset listed below are present in all people, but they are very common and create dysfunction in cultures:

- **Personal agendas:** being motivated solely by advancing one's own personal comfort, rather than a commitment to the team's agenda.
- **Assuming nefarious intent:** interpreting others' actions as reflecting an intention to do harm or be dishonest in some way.
- **Drama:** having an overblown reaction to situations.
- **Fixed mindset:** assuming that people's intelligence, behavior, capabilities, and even personality are fixed and that growth is not possible.
- **Judgmentalism:** having critical thoughts about others, either out loud or in our head.
- **Exclusion:** avoiding, ignoring, or rejecting someone or someone's input; this often produces silos or fiefdoms in organizations.
- **Retribution or fear of retribution:** having a fear of being fired, or simply being "punished" such as being shown a cold shoulder.
- **Conventionality:** doing something in a certain way because we've always done it that way.
- **Gossip and avoidance:** dodging discussion that could produce conflict, so if we're upset with someone we discuss it with someone else.
- **Powerlessness:** feeling that we lack the authority or capability to influence or impact our circumstances.
- **Incongruence:** saying one thing and doing another, such as professing a mission or values that we don't live up to
- **Blame:** defending or protecting ourselves by assigning fault to others.

The bottom line of all the above results in:

Resignation: giving up on the possibility that one can make an impact.

FEAR............................LOVE
CRITIC   EXECUTIVE

PERSONAL AGENDAS	▶	PERSONAL COMMITMENT
ASSUMING NEFARIOUS INTENT	▶	ASSUMING POSITIVE INTENT
DRAMA	▶	RADICAL ACCEPTANCE
FIXED MINDSET	▶	GROWTH MINDSET
JUDGMENTALISM	▶	ELEVATION
EXCLUSION	▶	INCLUSION
RETRIBUTION	▶	PSYCHOLOGICAL SAFETY
CONVENTIONALITY	▶	CREATIVITY
GOSSIP AND AVOIDANCE	▶	ACTIVE RESOLUTION
POWERLESSNESS	▶	AUTHORITY
INCONGRUENCE	▶	INTEGRITY
BLAME	▶	PERSONAL RESPONSIBILITY

FOCUS IS ON SELF	▶	FOCUS IS ON OTHERS

RESIGNATION	▶	*ENGAGEMENT*

When these mindsets are present in an organization, they erode the ability of any team to be as effective as possible. They have a direct impact on organizational results like quality of service, customer satisfaction, employee retention, and ultimately profitability. Poor results lead to more fear, and the cycle is made complete…and repeats.

That's the *vicious cycle.* And this vicious cycle happens unconsciously, without us making any deliberate decisions, because our amygdala puts us on autopilot. So we wake up with fear or anxiety that leads us to self-survival. We use our Default Success Strategy, which produces the personal and cultural mindsets we've just described. And those characteristics create a negative impact on the organization and its results. Then having terrible monthly profits or falling customer satisfaction ratings causes us to worry that we look bad or we might lose our job, so organizational outcomes such as burnout, stagnation, missional failure, or financial failure make us more afraid. And the cycle begins again…

As we said, the characteristics of our Default Success Strategy are completely natural and work great…until they don't. They can also be corrosive, both to the individual and to working as a team.

It's like water. Water is not a bad thing. It's clearly a very good thing, but it corrodes metal. That's just its nature. You can't change that—but you can rust-proof metal. And you can protect a team against corrosive characteristics by changing the vicious cycle into a virtuous cycle.

For purposes of being clear, we have depicted this vicious cycle as a linear progression from one state to the next, to the next. In fact, that's not the way it plays out. The cycle is more like an ecosystem of co-occurring states, each of which has an effect on others. The failure of a project can lead people to blame someone, which can cause the person blamed to double down on their Default Success Strategy of taking control. They organize a plan to turn the project around, but in the process are angry at those who blamed them and exercise some retribution, which produces more fear in others, which causes *them* to go into self-protection mode and become very dramatic as they gossip with others, rather than going to Joe to talk about the issue: "Joe has excluded me from this project because he is trying to make me the fall guy [assuming nefarious intent]."

We could go on, but you can see how cultures become toxic—and oftentimes very quickly. The point here is that the fear cycle happens unconsciously if intentional leadership isn't present. So let's talk about how leadership can disrupt this vicious cycle.

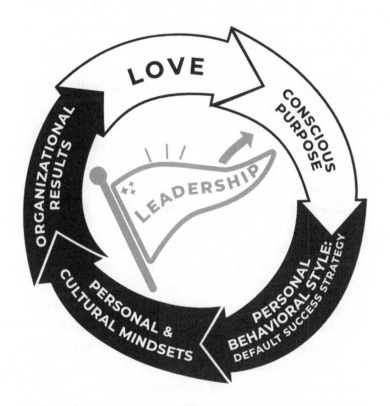

Your job as a leader is to use transformational leadership to intervene in this vicious cycle, shifting people from their unconscious purpose to a conscious purpose that's rooted in their desire to help other people. That's rooted in *love*.

We've discussed at some length what transformational leadership is. Now you can see how transforming people's purpose can lead them to consciously choose behaviors that are outside their Default Success Strategies—behaviors that we call *Conscious Success Strategies*. The conscious and skillful application of leadership, management, and coaching leads to a different mindset. We will delve into these tools more in Chapters 11 through 15, but for now just take note that creating a shift to the mindsets listed below is part of your job of creating a whole different disposition, both individually and as a culture:

- **Personal agendas** are replaced by **personal commitment** to an aspirational mission.
- **Assuming nefarious intent** is replaced by **assuming positive intent**: we interpret other people's words or actions in a constructive or optimistic way.
- **Drama** is replaced by **radical acceptance**: rather than complaining about conditions, we embrace them so we can figure out how to respond to them.
- **Fixed mindset** shifts to a **growth mindset**: we realize that we and others are capable of growing our intelligence, behavior, even attributes of our personality.
- **Judgmentalism** is replaced by **elevation**: rather than judging others as weak, incapable, or uncommitted, we assume they are resourceful and look to lift them up and help them be more effective.
- **Exclusion** is replaced by **inclusion**: we accept others who disagree with us or who come from significantly different backgrounds or cultures.
- **Retribution** is replaced by **psychological safety**: we contribute to others' growth or benefit by letting them express themselves and deliberately creating an environment where they feel free to speak up.
- **Conventionality** is replaced by **creativity**: we take the risk of trying new things because we are more committed to our organization's purpose than we are to being safe.
- **Gossip and avoidance** are replaced by **active resolution**: if we

have issues, we put them on the table and talk about them to resolve them.

- **Powerlessness** is replaced by **authority** that is proportionate to responsibility.
- **Incongruence** is replaced by **integrity**: we do what we say we're going to do.
- **Blame** is replaced by **personal responsibility and supportive accountability**: we don't ask "Who is to blame?" but "How am I responsible for fixing or changing this? And how can I use supportive accountability to help others?"

The bottom line of all these shifts is that:

Resignation is replaced by **engagement**: people possess an aspirational purpose and feel empowered to exercise their judgment or influence toward its accomplishment.

PERSONAL AGENDAS ⋯⋯▶	PERSONAL COMMITMENT
ASSUMING NEFARIOUS INTENT ⋯⋯▶	ASSUMING POSITIVE INTENT
DRAMA ⋯⋯▶	RADICAL ACCEPTANCE
FIXED MINDSET ⋯⋯▶	GROWTH MINDSET
JUDGMENTALISM ⋯⋯▶	ELEVATION
EXCLUSION ⋯⋯▶	INCLUSION
RETRIBUTION ⋯⋯▶	PSYCHOLOGICAL SAFETY
CONVENTIONALITY ⋯⋯▶	CREATIVITY
GOSSIP AND AVOIDANCE ⋯⋯▶	ACTIVE RESOLUTION
POWERLESSNESS ⋯⋯▶	AUTHORITY
INCONGRUENCE ⋯⋯▶	INTEGRITY
BLAME ⋯⋯▶	PERSONAL RESPONSIBILITY
FOCUS IS ON SELF ⋯⋯▶	FOCUS IS ON OTHERS
RESIGNATION ⋯⋯▶	*ENGAGEMENT*

The Cultural Mindsets™

Shifting to these twelve mindsets yields a whole different set of organizational results:

- Instead of **burnout**, people are **energized**.
- Instead of **stagnation**, people are **growing**.
- Instead of **diminishing** value, value is **increasing**.
- **Missional failure** is replaced by **missional success**.
- **Financial failure** is replaced by **financial sustainability**.

Again, it's a series of day-by-day, moment-by-moment choices. And again, it's a self-reinforcing cycle.

The more people see that we have successes and the better we do, the more it leads to us focusing on others and the more it leads to us feeling secure. That means we can now look out for what's best for our customers or associates, which reinforces our conscious purpose. And so that virtuous cycle begins again...

TRANSFORMATION TO THE VIRTUOUS CYCLE

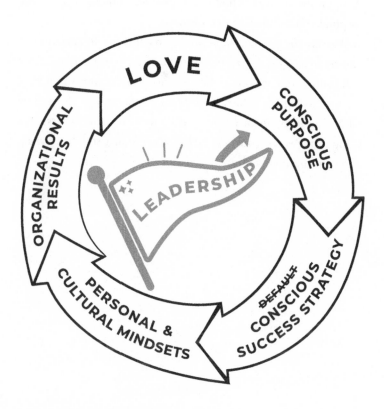

TRANSFORMING YOU

Transformation begins with *you*. If you're going to be a transformational leader, you have to inspire your leadership team so that you and they can lead the broader culture. If you are going to be a transformational leader, it needs to start with you being able to lead your own life, being able to transform your own mindset.

When you wake up with those fears, you need to be able to shift to "I'm on a mission today. I've got a higher purpose today." That will eclipse the fears. They won't go away, but they will largely get replaced in your psyche so that now they coexist with a higher purpose and you can choose which state you're going to be in. Without the ability to choose, you can't lead others. If you're not inspired yourself, how do you inspire other people?

You are the engine, the power source in your organization. If you are in a vicious cycle, motivated by fear, your team members will follow. But if you are in a virtuous cycle, motivated by a mission to benefit others, your team members will also follow. Choosing to be inspired by your commitment to others, and being aware when your fear kicks in, is the first step in creating a transformational culture.

CHAPTER 4

LEARNED FORGETFULNESS

"I know that I exist; the question is, what is this 'I' that 'I' know?"

—René Descartes

You aren't who you think you are. And chances are you aren't who other people think you are, either.

Our self-image is based primarily on how we've behaved in the past, and although our past has helped shape us, it doesn't have to define us.

We'll investigate this a bit more, but first we should acknowledge that our approach flies in the face of many aspects of conventional psychology. We've heard psychologists (not to mention HR professionals and coaches) talk about an individual's behavioral profile, such as Myers Briggs or DISC, as if they define a person.

The problem is that most of these types of profiles can only be based on who we *were*. **What is far more important is *who we can be*.** Leaders are called to a higher purpose and therefore a higher level of behavior, which means we can never just say, "This is who I am." We must continue to grow.

COMMITMENT COUNTS

We are all informed by our past, but we're not restricted by our past…unless we choose to be.

The accumulation of what we've learned from our past gets imprinted on our emotional mind and makes us unconsciously competent at being one way or another. We revert to behavior that has helped us in situations before, and it becomes automatic and comfortable. A person who reacts to stress by being very aggressive is unconsciously competent at being aggressive. They needn't think about acting aggressively; it comes easily to them. Someone who is very quiet is unconsciously competent at being very quiet. And so on.

It's like riding a bicycle. While we're cycling, we're unconsciously competent at balancing. Balance is so automatic, unconscious, and comfortable that trying to unbalance is almost impossible.

Part of who we are is the accumulation of our past, but we are also our commitment to the future, our higher purpose. Like the shy parent who was unconsciously competent at remaining silent but who was inspired by her commitment to her child's future and spoke out at the PTA meeting. Her intervention is motivated by creating the best possible future for her child, not about her personal comfort.

Or like Isaiah, the engineer from the inner city whose experience could have relegated him to a difficult life, all too common among his neighborhood peers. He saw an alternate possible future for himself: being an architect, owning a firm, living well, sending his kids to good schools, helping disadvantaged youth.

And he committed to that future. That commitment had a greater impact on what Isaiah became than the experiences from his past.

Commitment is so important we've dedicated a whole chapter to it (see Chapter 6). But it may be useful for you to begin to start thinking now about what's the inspiring commitment that motivates you.

A DEFENSE OF HYPOCRISY

That's right, hypocrisy.

An essential part of transformation is what may appear to be hypocrisy: imagining that we are something we are not. But in this case, we are not simply pretending to have more laudable values than we actually have, which is simple deception. **We are trying to live up to unattained aspiration; we are espousing a high moral standard but failing to live up to it, not because of an intent to deceive, but because living up to high standards is *really* difficult.** If we set our goals high enough, we are almost bound to fail to reach them sometimes. But isn't it better to have standards and sometimes fail to achieve them than to not have standards at all?

When we're striving to achieve a goal, whether in our personal or work life, but we haven't gotten there yet, it's helpful to not think of ourselves as hypocrites because that will limit our commitment. Rather, think of ourselves as always striving—and be proud of ourselves...and keep striving!

No one would criticize a kid who at a very young age decides he wants to become a football player, even though he trips over his own shoelaces. He starts playing and is lousy, but he improves and gets stronger, and he keeps playing. Then he goes to the next level and the next level. Maybe he starts playing little league football, then high school, then college...then he might aspire to become a professional football player. His aspiration is not fake or hypocritical. He's committed to it, no matter how unachievable it initially seemed—or might still be.

We can all do the same. Commit to a purpose or a behavior, and then exercise it and develop it. If your first reaction is to snap at people, try keeping your mouth shut and smiling. If your instinct is to keep quiet, try speaking up. It feels awkward. But it's just like a kid that learns to run a button hook pattern on the football field. The kid runs downfield and does an abrupt about-face. It's very awkward and uncomfortable until you become accustomed to the movement—but it's not being fake. It's developing a new behavior.

That's what transformation is all about.

Brad's grandfather was born in 1883, and he got educated through the eighth grade. By the time he graduated, he had all of the knowledge and all the skills he needed to live his life. He ran a butcher shop but went broke in the Depression. He then went to work at a box factory. He owned a small house and raised a couple of kids.

Then Brad's father came along, was in the military, and went to college. He learned a whole new set of information and behaviors that his father didn't have. And he had a very successful career and life using what he learned as a young man.

So, in the past, we've learned from generation to generation. But in this day and age, society and the economy are changing so fast, because of the availability of information and technology, that we graduate college with enough information to last for maybe a decade. **Then we have to retool ourselves repeatedly throughout our lives to keep up with this rapidly changing world.** This behavioral agility will be crucial to success for leaders over the coming decades.

This rapid transformation is a new model for the development of the human species: not Darwin's intergenerational model but an *intra*-generational model. We're going to need more of this ability as we live longer into the future. The time horizon in which our knowledge and behaviors become obsolete is getting shorter and shorter as time goes on. We will all need to transform ourselves multiple times.

As we saw in the last chapter, as the leader, you are the engine that needs to lead these uncomfortable changes. That's your role on behalf of your team. The good news is that once you introduce transformation to your organization, it starts to spread, first from you to your executive team, then from them to other leaders, and so on out into the whole organization.

That process depends on one vital fact: *everyone can change.*

We present this statement as fact. You may see it differently.

CHAPTER 5

THE POSSIBILITY
OF CHANGE

"The measure of intelligence is the ability to change."

—ALBERT EINSTEIN

We'd love to tell you all our client teams greet us, ready to embrace our approach to organizational and personal growth. But in thirty years, we've encountered our share of skepticism.

For some, in fact, skepticism would have been an upgrade.

One such skeptic was the chief financial officer of a healthcare firm who spent the entire two-and-a-half-day workshop with his back to us. He just sat there reading printouts, or pretending to read them, to signal to the entire executive team that he wasn't buying into our nonsense.

Our approach? We left the CFO alone. Clearly, he wasn't ready for our brand of change. We guessed that he was all about the tactical, the managerial, processes, protocols. Not that he said so much. He would barely speak with us.

We finished that workshop, and everybody but the CFO professed that they'd gotten huge value from it. As we always do, we spent the next several months conducting coaching sessions with the executive team, individually and as a group. After one session, Brad happened to walk past the CFO's office, and waved at him.

The CFO came out to the hall and said haltingly, "I have to say, I'm amazed at the changes around here. We're addressing things that I've been complaining about and worried about for years, things I never dreamed we'd be addressing." Moreover, he explained that these changes were having an impact on business. The firm's membership started to do a 180...growing instead of shrinking.

Now that the CFO had witnessed growth with his own two eyes, he could no longer deny that this stuff works. He became a fan, and his enthusiasm further boosted the success of the program for the whole company.

While it wasn't easy speaking to someone's back for two and a half days—frankly, it was weird—we didn't hold his skepticism against him. We've run into resistance to coaching for three decades now, and we understand why. Most of what's done in the team-building, leadership-development space is just not effective. And the idea that people can fundamentally change how they behave—their personality—is something that so few have experienced that it seems unattainable. But change is necessary. In the words of Albert Einstein, *"We cannot solve our problems with the same thinking we used when we created them."*

CHANGE IS POSSIBLE

Some programs work. And once you witness these results, or experience them yourself, you start to see that change is possible. In 1991, Brad was in his mid-thirties and had been a two-pack-a-day smoker for eighteen years—half his life. Then he completed a weekend-long self-improvement course, walked out to his car, put his cigarettes in the glovebox...and he hasn't smoked since.

So he knew change was possible. He had seen the power of transformational work personally—and he could see the possibilities of using such an approach in leadership programs to help people grow.

It wasn't just smoking. Brad experienced all kinds of personal breakthroughs that helped him understand the high level of frustration and unhappiness in his life. A year later, he sold the family business and became one of the country's first coaches.

It seemed to him that the best place to fuel transformation in people's lives is at work. Work is where people spend most of their waking time—working with others. The best way to achieve change is in a community of people that can support one another—today we call it a culture, but the phrase didn't exist at the time. The other advantage of working with organizations is that it was easy to measure the results of personal transformation in the organization's performance.

NO ONE IS FIXED IN STONE

Brad's experience is clear evidence that transformation can be positive—and yet skepticism remains a constant among people who have not experienced personal transformation for themselves.

When we introduce the idea, the reaction we run into over and over again is, "But this is just the way I am. This is the way I'm wired."

It's more pronounced in some cultures than others. We once worked with a digital marketing group in England, a group of about twenty truly brilliant people, but it brought us into head-on conflict with the British class system. Perhaps we should have guessed when we were invited to hold an evening meeting at the home of the CEO, a duke who lived in a castle. When we raised the possibility of a higher purpose that could help people grow, the whole room erupted. It was like one of those scenes in the British Parliament when everyone is shouting everyone else down. We just stood there asking, "What the heck just happened?"

One gentleman complained that he couldn't envisage a higher purpose for himself because they were all kept in their boxes by the class system or the work hierarchy, and offering them *all* the possibility of a higher purpose was in direct conflict with the norms of British culture. At one point he said, "I'm only a C3. I can't have a higher purpose." Interestingly, these norms were a holdover from the class system, which had been abolished decades earlier…but the vestiges of the past still held them in "their place," like Mr. Eisenhower's tiger, Mohini.

At one point, after an engaging but very uncomfortable exercise, it all got too much for Andrew, the VP of Sales. He had been resistant throughout the program, and this particular exercise was the last straw. He stormed out, shouting, "I can't take any more of this!"

His reaction underlines our point that humans tend to see

themselves as fixed (*"It's just the way I am."*). We've already described how our Default Success Strategy limits how we react to situations, so we feel more comfortable always reacting the same way. But we don't have to be limited by our unconscious motivations. It's not who we are. Our Default Success Strategy is a strategy we've adopted. It's the behavior we automatically go to without thinking consciously about it, but it's not inevitable. It's not fixed within us. We can learn to behave in different ways. Case in point: our angry VP of Sales, Andrew, came back the next day and, after reflecting, realized how fixed he had become, and voluntarily identified some growth targets for himself!

A lot of people we coach have done personality type tests: Myers-Briggs, or Predictive Index, or Enneagram, or the Color Personality Test. They're meant to give a snapshot of the personalities in an organization, and they can be useful for helping people understand themselves and others—but they tend to be interpreted by people in a way that concretizes their behavior rather than making them more flexible. Individuals learn to think of themselves as "fixed": they are a "director," "interactor," "moderator," "disruptor," and so on. People get categorized.

We've seen people who have their four-letter Myers-Briggs type on their office nameplate. The message is, "That's just how I am, right? You know what you're getting when you walk in here."

As soon as you're defined by "This is who I am," you've put yourself inside a box. You've limited your potential.

No one is fixed like that. Everyone can change…and grow. Years before he got into the coaching business, Brad took a behavioral profile that told him he had "low sociability." The people he worked with went, "Ah, okay, we get it. That's why he doesn't care about people." Brad was frustrated, because he *knew* that he wasn't unsociable; he simply had a lower need for interaction. He decided that if he made more of an effort to interact with people, they would see that he did care about them—and that would make him a better leader.

The people who ran the profile told him there was no way to change his "natural behavior." Brad thought, *I'll show you! Just watch me*—which is around the time he started thinking about what limits the way we behave, which eventually led to the idea of the Default Success Strategy.

Anyone can grow and get outside their box. But to do that, *you first have to realize that you're in a box.*

SCIENTIFIC BACKING

You don't have to take our word that everyone has the power to change. When we started this work, there was little scientific research to back it up. In fact, we used to joke that it was magic! Today, that explanation has been replaced by an ever-growing body of research. Stanford Professor Carol Dweck's 2012 book *Mindset: How You Can Fulfill Your Potential* explores the concept that, while most of us fundamentally believe our intelligence and capabilities are fixed, **generating a different mindset actually opens us up to the possibility of growing**. We can actually increase and shape our intelligence as we go through life, developing new behaviors and approaches. Dweck's fundamental premise is now well known, and it has been proved in study after study.

NEUROPLASTICITY: IT'S TIME TO CHANGE

Another influential book, *The Mind and the Brain: Neuroplasticity and the Power of Mental Force*, by Jeffrey M. Schwartz and Sharon Begley, discussed the then-new concept of neuroplasticity. That book documented studies disproving a popular old belief. For years, people thought the amount of brain and nerve tissue we had was fixed during adolescence, and if we suffered brain or nerve damage, we were in serious trouble because it was unable to regenerate.

Well, that turned out to be false, as Schwartz and Begley highlighted. More recent studies have found that, in fact, brain tissue is constantly regenerating. The brain is like a muscle: the more we put it under stress, the more it grows.

Psychologist Daniel Goleman, who coined the term "emotional intelligence," identified eight different types of intelligence—and stressed that we all have the ability consciously to increase our intelligence in all the different types.

Neuroplasticity refers to the ability of the brain's neural networks—the synapses and neurons—to create new pathways. In other words, our brain can learn new ways to think in response to demand and stress.

Consider the way a golfer can "groove" a new, improved swing. That's the brain learning new patterns.

Or take another example. Say you're right-handed, but you break your right arm and force yourself to learn to write with your left hand. It will be difficult, and awkward, and it'll take you some time to become proficient—but with enough repetition, your brain will develop new pathways, and you'll develop this ability.

THE POWER OF THE UNCONSCIOUS

Humans' ability to change is well documented, but the problem we face in overcoming skepticism about change is that the unconscious mind is incredibly powerful. In his book *The Social Animal,* author David Brooks cites a researcher at the University of Virginia who determined that the unconscious mind can handle more than 11 million pieces of data at any given time. Not only is our unconscious brain managing our heart rate, blood pressure, kidneys, and so on; it knows how much light is in the room in which we're sitting (and thus the approximate time of day), what music is playing, whether the dog just walked out of the room, whether we're hungry or thirsty, all while reading a book and thinking through the applications of what we're reading…a remarkable quantity of variables.

By comparison, our *conscious* mind can handle—wait for it—a puny forty or so pieces of data at once.

No wonder it's a challenge to train our unconscious minds to change.

Brooks argues that people are primarily products of their

unconscious minds. This part of our brain largely determines our behavior and the decisions that we make.

Every time you hear someone say, "I'm just not comfortable with that," it's another way of saying, "That scares me, so I'm not going to do it." But because the fear is at a level below what we're conscious of, we just think the suggestion was a bad idea.

For us, the neuroscientific and psychological breakthroughs of recent decades have only confirmed what we already knew: that personal transformation is possible. In many ways, it reinforces the stories of the ages. The great religions are full of stories of people who have been converted or changed their path in life, and who have been transformed by gaining faith. Many of the great novelists of the past, from Charles Dickens and Leo Tolstoy to Saul Bellow and Philip Roth, describe how characters undergo dramatic growth over the course of the story.

Most people implicitly understand that it is possible to change our behavior throughout their life—though because it is usually very hard, we often find it easier to envisage others changing rather than ourselves. But the research makes it easier for us to convince people that they can fundamentally change their behavior for the better.

CULTURE EATS EVERYTHING

Around the world, billions of dollars are spent every year on culture change efforts, and most of that money is wasted. And even more money is wasted on strategic plans that make no meaningful difference.

Unfortunately, this is not a new phenomenon. Decades ago, the phrase "Culture eats strategy for breakfast" came into being (and has since been attributed to the legendary management consultant and writer Peter Drucker). This quote speaks to the importance of both culture and strategy within any effective organization while showing that culture is far more influential than strategy. We believe this to be true, but we would argue that **culture** is so powerful that it **eats everything** for breakfast, lunch, and dinner. The most successful businesses, schools, and organizations of all kinds deeply understand this and spend most of their energy on constantly improving their culture.

WINNING OVER THE SKEPTICS

Most, if not all, CEOs have been through leadership training. And many CEOs and leaders have been through workshops, ropes courses, trust falls, and the like and have seen the benefits of such work disappear in short order. This creates understandable skepticism.

Remember our favorite skeptic from the beginning of the chapter? The CFO who spent two days showing us his back? He became not only a convert but a long-term friend; we see him around town and have met his family. He now says:

> When we began this process, I knew in my heart of hearts that this was going to be a complete waste of time and that none of my team-mates would change the behaviors that I had seen as a problem for a long time. So I was actually angry that we were wasting this time. I carried this attitude through the entire workshop and for about a month afterward, at which point I began to see substantial change in the behavior of my teammates. They stepped up to responsibilities and went to work on increasing their effectiveness. I began to see

major improvements in our service and our financial status. I have to say, I'm a true believer now, and sorry I was so cynical.

This approach works. It's not about woo-woo or drum circles or singing "Kumbaya." It is the wisdom of the ages, passed down by the ancients and virtually all religious and spiritual teachings, confirmed by psychology, cognitive research, and organizations that have pulled off transformations they'd thought impossible.

At this stage, by the way, we should note that there's a difference between skepticism and cynicism. *Skepticism* is a critical questioning of a claim, and that kind of questioning is at the heart of effectiveness and even innovation. *Cynicism* is complete pessimism, an unexamined dismissal of a possibility without any critical examination. While skepticism is a function of the thinking mind, cynicism is a function of the emotional mind and arises from fear.

In the next chapter, we'll explore commitment and its vital role in organizational growth.

CHAPTER 6

COMMITMENT

"Whenever the early Christians entered a town, the power structure got disturbed... They were small in number but big in commitment. They were too God-intoxicated to be 'astronomically intimidated.' They brought an end to such ancient evils as infanticide and gladiatorial contest."

—MARTIN LUTHER KING, JR.

Many culture change models are based on extrinsic motivation. In other words, they offer this or that improvement in performance as an incentive for putting in the work. If you change this or that behavior, for example, your reward will be increased sales and greater profitability.

Transformational Leadership also generates motivation—but it's *intrinsic* motivation. Commitment drives a deeper, more enduring transformation. People get energized by some inspiring purpose to which they commit themselves.

As humans, we often find it quite easy to get motivated to fix a problem we have. Once the problem is fixed, however, the motivation wanes and we return to our old behaviors. That's because motivation is a short-term emotional impulse. Our emotional motivation, just like our emotions themselves, comes and goes. It's seldom consistent.

We get motivated to lose weight because our doctor explains the consequences of being overweight, and that makes us afraid. So we change our behaviors for a while and think, *Okay, that's fixed.* Then we slide back into comfortable habits, and we gain the weight back.

Personal transformation is much different than that. Personal transformation comes about when we commit to a purpose that excites us, a vision for the future that motivates our actions. Every January, gyms fill up with swarms of enthusiastic clients motivated by excessive feasting during the holiday season or by the tradition of New Year's resolutions. We swear to hit the gym/treadmill/bike three times a week…and this time, we mean it (unlike last time, and the time before, and the time before that).

By March 1, most are a distant memory. We won't be back in the gym for another ten months.

Instead of being motivated to hit the gym three times a week to lose that problem weight, we would have been better off committing to working out regularly, even if it's only for ten minutes each week.

That's what Tom did a few years ago. He made a commitment to exercise at least three times a week. It took some time, but he's noticed that now he doesn't have to get himself motivated every week. He made the decision once to work out, and thus he doesn't have to make that decision again. The power of commitment means that he works out even on days when he really doesn't want to, because he never has to ask himself the question, "Do I feel like working out today?"

Tom's commitment is part of a higher commitment to his health, to setting an example for his kids, and to being able to perform at his best for his clients. Seen like that, working out is a small part of a larger, transformative commitment to providing a loving contribution to others in his life.

People who are *motivated* to lose weight lose some weight... and then go back to their old habits. People who *commit* to their health make substantial changes in their behavior and lifestyle. This commitment to a quality healthspan (a healthy life span) fundamentally alters one's daily decisions.

Commitment can sound complicated but, in fact, once you make a commitment, things become easier. Once you make a fundamental shift from being motivated by your emotions to being motivated by a higher commitment, committing to the small stuff is simple.

You might protest, "I've committed many times to working out, but I haven't been able to follow through on that commitment." That's because we often confuse committing to do something with committing to *try* to do something. A commitment to try is tentative and is contingent on our emotional state, the circumstances, other people's opinions, and lots of factors. A commitment to do something has no contingency. It's like a commitment to make a mortgage payment. No banker will accept it if you say, "I'll try to repay that loan."

We're not saying there's anything wrong with a try; trying is good. But the whole point is that many people don't think in terms of making commitments, especially to themselves. They don't see their behavior in terms of their higher purpose. Our answer to that is that a commitment to yourself is as valuable as a commitment to others. If you can't keep a commitment to yourself, don't make a commitment. But don't pretend you're making a commitment when you're actually only committing to trying.

As Yoda said, "There is no try. There is only do."

COMMITMENT VS. MOTIVATION

"Commitment is what transforms a promise into reality."

—ABRAHAM LINCOLN

Motivation comes and goes, but commitment endures. Motivation gets you excited, but commitment makes things happen. Motivation can be fuzzy and gray; commitment is black and white.

Take marriage. For many people, the motivation for getting married will come and go. That feeling of inspired, overwhelming romantic love isn't there every minute of every day—but we've made a commitment, so we stand by our partner even when motivation flags. We'll work through conflict, we'll resist the temptation to pursue others, because we made a commitment in front of family and friends, and exchanged wedding bands to signify that commitment.

If a marriage falls apart, it's frequently because the people involved have been led by their emotions, their fears.

The institution of marriage has endured thousands of years. So when we talk about commitment versus motivation, we're not talking about some new-age concept. We're talking about wisdom that has survived generations.

It's the same as religious faith. Once we commit to a belief in a faith—whatever that faith might be—then that belief simply is. There may be days when our emotions make us more frustrated that our life is not perfect or our ambitions are not coming true; there may be days when the news is full of stories of terrible things, and our emotions make us very upset—but true faith endures. Our commitment stands up in the face of whatever we endure.

COMMITMENT WORKS

One of our favorite quotations, attributed to the German romantic poet Goethe in the early 1800s, explains the transformational effect of commitment:

> Until one is committed, there is hesitancy, the chance to draw back, always ineffectiveness. Concerning all acts of initiative (and creation), there is one elementary truth the ignorance of which kills countless ideas and splendid plans: that the moment one definitely commits oneself, then providence moves too. A whole stream of events issues from the decision, raising in one's favour all manner of unforeseen incidents, meetings and material assistance, which no man could have dreamt would have come his way. Whatever you can do or dream you can, begin it. Boldness has genius, power, and magic in it!

Generating and evoking from people a **personal commitment** to a higher purpose that stirs their heart is a distinguishing feature of transformational leadership. It must be done every day in every discussion. It is very different from simply creating a vision or mission statement and going on to the next task.

COURAGE TO LEAD

Commitment to leadership demands courage, as anyone in a leadership role knows. Leadership comes with risk. Any leader may have to make decisions that are unpopular, or even extremely challenging (like firing someone), or that put the company at risk financially or reputationally.

To engage in transformational leadership is doubly difficult because it requires us continually speaking about our higher purpose. It frequently evokes worries that people will think you a dreamer, or that you have an overinflated sense of your importance, or that people will dismiss you as corny, or an unrealistic idealist; that's inherently frightening, and it requires courage.

Nearly fifty years ago, the psychologist Rollo May said, "Courage is not a virtue or value among other personal values like love or fidelity. It is the foundation that underlies and gives reality to all other virtues and personal values.

"The word courage comes from the same stem as the French word *coeur*, meaning 'heart.' Thus, just as one's heart, by pumping blood to one's arms, legs, and brain enables all the other physical organs to function, so courage makes possible all the psychological virtues.

"Without courage, other values wither away into mere facsimiles of virtue."

May teaches us that courage is required to live out our values, our aspirations, and our faith and is the first essential ingredient for impactful leadership.

LEAP OF FAITH

One of our first clients in the behavioral health field was a regional Medicaid funder. While working with the executive team, the CEO began speaking about her commitment to Integrated Health (this was back in 2002, before Integrated Health was common). We looked at her quizzically—and so did her team. But after she explained how the integration of mental health and physical health care could benefit their customers and society as a whole, everyone in the room committed to her approach.

The implementation of integrated care, however, required a change in the state funding laws, something most CEOs of such organizations wouldn't even consider possible. However, this CEO made an appointment with the State Attorney General, convinced him that the law needed to be changed, and got it done. Within two years, the organization had seven Integrated Health sites within the county it served.

Not only did the CEO need to change the law, but she also needed to convince her team, local officials, and the Primary Health Care organizations she partnered with that this newfangled concept was valid enough to be worth the pain of making major changes to their treatment model and business models. Decades later, many organizations in the field are still talking about implementing integrated health care—but are resigned to the status quo because they lack the courage to lead the necessary growth.

Courage is not the same as being fearless or reckless. It's not the same as ignoring warnings and dangers. It's a conscious decision to overcome our fears and concerns and take a calculated risk. It's active, not passive. Human beings *have* fear. We *do* courage. It's something we all get to choose.

Think about someone doing a bungee jump for the first time. Rationally, they know that the bridge on which they're standing is sound, that the cord is sturdy and recently inspected, its metal clasps professionally fastened. They know they'll be fine.

And yet…stepping out onto the ledge and stepping off requires courage. It is a leap of faith.

The work we explore in this book will require a similar leap of faith.

BRINGING OTHERS ALONG

If we want to be at the very top level of CEOs, we must strive to transform more than just ourselves—we must bring these ideas to life for our team.

When Tom was pursuing his MBA at Notre Dame, he spoke to one of his trusted advisors about how important humility was to him. The advisor told him, "I know you want to commit your life to God, to serving others and being an example, but you can't do that by playing small." Another professor added that sloth was one of the seven deadly sins. That hit Tom like a thunderbolt. He worked out, he ran, he studied hard. He had never thought of himself as slothful—but the professor brought attention to the idea that any failure to use one's God-given talents may be a form of slothfulness.

Tom began to realize that he had focused too much on his own humility and not enough on using his gifts to help others. The Hebrew root of the word *humility* means "to take up your God-given space in the world." In other words, you accept what you've been given and use it fully.

In the words of the author Marianne Williamson, "Your playing small does not serve the world. There is nothing enlightened about shrinking so that other people won't feel insecure around you. We are all meant to shine, as children do. We were born to make manifest the glory of God that is within us."

Like us, you have been given gifts, whether or not you credit them to God, talent, education, opportunities, or other reasons. If you truly want to bring about transformative change in your organization, it's incumbent on you to use these gifts to help others. As CEOs and leaders, we have a responsibility to, well, lead people. *It's our job.*

You may never have dreamed of achieving the role you have achieved, but here you are. To not do your utmost to improve the culture would be playing small, and that would be downright irresponsible.

By starting to read this book, you've demonstrated interest and initiative. Before we begin the next chapter, where you'll begin to discover your higher purpose, we would ask that you, too, pause to make a conscious mental commitment to the openness and effort required for the process. While you consider it, keep in mind these words:

> The moment one definitely commits oneself, then providence moves too.

> It's time to move providence.

CHAPTER 7

YOUR UNCONSCIOUS PURPOSE

"In virtually all the great spiritual and philosophical traditions of the world, there appears some form of the idea that most human beings are sleepwalking through their own existence."

—NATHANIEL BRANDEN

When we met Caroline, she was the Human Resources Director at a Human Services Organization. We learned that she had taken a fascinating path into HR. A person of deep religious beliefs, she studied at the seminary, where she found herself talking with a friend who was contemplating suicide. Caroline talked the friend out of taking her life, and helped her find ongoing professional counseling.

Caroline realized not only that she enjoyed such counseling and was good at it—but that it was her calling in life. She changed her major to Christian counseling and, after graduation, became a licensed social worker. She excelled and was promoted into other positions focused on helping people before starting to make her way up the HR pyramid…to the top.

It was clear from her story that Caroline had a very big heart, a strong sense of purpose, and a powerful belief in God. After all, she had made a conscious decision to devote her life and career to helping others. So you'll be as surprised as we were—and as she was—that her peers described her in evaluations as a cold-hearted—well, let's say it—"witch."

What?

To explore the mismatch between others' evaluations and what we knew about Caroline, we helped her look deeper. As it turned out, Caroline's Default Success Strategy lay at the root of the matter.

Caroline had a high need for perfection. When looking into an issue, she would undertake exhaustive research, which is a common trait among excellent HR administrators and financial professionals. She feared nothing more than going off half-cocked, so she double- and triple-checked facts and figures to ensure that when the time came to make a decision, she had the right answer. On one hand, this caused her to excel at her job: risk management, documenting policies and procedures to support effective recruiting and hiring—all the detail-oriented functions that are critical to HR administration. On the other hand, her belief that there was one right answer to every question caused her to view the world in very black-and-white terms. As it turned out, her desperation to be right—to cross all the t's and dot every last i—came across as judgmental and condescending to her team members.

When we shared peer evaluations with Caroline, she was devastated. Deep research into any given question or decision had served her well during her steady climb to a senior position.

We'll come back to how Caroline reacted to the news, but what she and most leaders need to understand is this:

Your Default Success Strategy becomes your purpose, unconsciously!

In this case, Caroline's purpose in everything she did was to ensure correctness and perfection *according to her definition*. This unconscious purpose served her well in some situations—numbers, writing policies, ensuring procedures are documented and followed—and it undermined her effectiveness in other situations, namely leading people.

In other words:

" OUR DEFAULT SUCCESS STRATEGY WORKS GREAT...

UNTIL IT DOESN'T!
"

DEFAULT SUCCESS STRATEGY™

The key to understanding your Default Success Strategy™ is right there in the words.

Default. It's natural. It's your go-to. You never have to think about it. If a bowl of Raisin Bran is your default breakfast, mornings are easy; you've one less decision to make. And as we said earlier, taking away decisions makes our brains happy.

Success. You've done well in your career and, chances are, in life. If you hadn't enjoyed success already, you wouldn't be reading this book to build upon it. It's important to keep this in mind because success actually makes it harder to change things up, to grow. And the more you embrace your strengths, the more success you'll have.

Strategy. The tools you've used thus far to achieve what you've achieved comprise a strategy. At some level beneath the threshold of consciousness, you understand that your behaviors have served you well and may continue to do so.

Often, people take a dim view of their own Default Success Strategy once they are introduced to it. Their assumption is that, because it's the path they naturally follow, it can't possibly be good enough. Just as the grass is always greener on the other side of the fence, our peers' strategies may look more fruitful than ours.

We discourage such thinking. Success is success, and your strategy has produced plenty for you. What we want you to realize is that your Default Success Strategy does not define you; it is not *you*. In some situations it is an asset in the pursuit of your higher purpose, and in other situations it impedes your higher purpose.

Your Default Success Strategy works great...until it doesn't!

TOO EASYGOING

One CEOs is a very friendly, easygoing, affable man. He is dearly loved by his staff of almost 1,000 people. His Default Success Strategy was all about being of service, ensuring people were comfortable, caring for them. He inspired people with his acts of service and his gentle approach to ensuring everyone was comfortable, and his orientation toward service and helping others pervaded the organization. He was an inspiring leader, but the only situation in which his Default Success Strategy didn't work was when he needed to hold people accountable. He constantly let people off the hook because he didn't want them, or himself, to be uncomfortable. The result in some cases was poor service, a lack of innovation, and disappointing financial outcomes. Remember, he didn't do any of this consciously. This was his unconscious, automatic behavior.

It worked great (for building relationships)...*until it didn't* (for creating accountability for results).

There's a good chance that the reason you're reading this book is that you've reached a career plateau of sorts where your comfy old set of tools is no longer providing the growth you'd like. Take heart: you *can* jump-start that growth. Remember that we make a choice to exercise our Default Success Strategy. It's just that we make this choice unconsciously.

Well, what's to prevent you from replacing your unconscious choices with conscious ones?

Not a thing.

FEAR AND LEADING

Just as our devoted Raisin Bran fan doesn't wake up wondering whether they'll make an omelet, you probably seldom arise thinking, *Gee, I guess I'll stay in my comfort zone today.* Rather, using your Default Success Strategy to stay in your comfort zone is automatic and unconscious. It actually becomes a purpose to work toward.

Whether we are aware of it or not, our unconscious purpose is always rooted in fear. It's about not wanting to operate outside our comfort zone. Sometimes if you propose something to a colleague, they might respond, "I'm not comfortable with that." That's not quite the same as saying, "That's a bad idea," or "That's a good idea." In fact, a colleague might say, "That's a really good idea, but I'm not comfortable with it." Sound familiar?

"I'm not comfortable with that" is a deodorized way of saying, "That scares me." It's the things outside our comfort zone that frighten us, because we perceive them as entailing risk, and everyone wants to reduce risk. We all want to operate in a way we're familiar and *comfortable* with.

Caroline, our HR manager, was constantly (and unconsciously) worried about being shown to be inept, or incapable, or lacking knowledge. So she went to remarkable lengths to support her arguments, doing endless Internet research and gathering all available evidence to help make a decision. But when she made her decision, she would go home for the night...and she would wake up the next morning wondering, *Well, maybe that wasn't the right decision.* Second-guessing herself, she would return to the office and research some more, gathering still more evidence until she had an airtight case.

Because Caroline was scared of being viewed as inept, anybody who tried to argue with her was threatening her sense of personal capability. So she would argue them down by showing them reference after reference, citing source after source. The message, as others perceived it, was that Caroline had an inarguable answer to whatever the issue was: *"I'm right and you're wrong."*

Caroline lost sight of the feelings of others; her sole goal became to prove that her answer or recommendation was correct. People got bruised—and she didn't even realize it until she got the feedback from her 360-leadership survey.

Her Default Success Strategy (precise facts) *worked great…until it didn't* (bruised relationships).

She got a chance to change her behavior—and we'll tell you in the next chapter how she grasped it with both hands.

KNOW YOUR OWN DEFAULTS

Now that we've explored the concept of Default Success Strategy in more depth, we can begin to do some tough work to discover: *What is yours?* It's relatively easy to see what makes others tick. But as a leader, you need to fully understand yourself before you can help the rest of your team or organization. Just as the flight attendant instructs passengers to put on their own oxygen mask first, we're asking you to take care of your own needs before you can help others.

Whether you're a CEO or in some other leadership role, you play a major role in the social dynamic that creates your company culture. Your personal Default Success Strategy is reflected in the organization, whether you realize it or not. **To grow company culture, you must first grow yourself.**

Once you begin this work, you will initially be surprised at how these shifts in your behavior are soon reflected throughout the organization.

The CEO is so central to the success of any culture change effort that we don't engage with the effort unless it begins with the CEO.

TIME TO ELEVATE

Yes, it's time to elevate—and we mean that in more ways than one. Now that we've explored the concept of the Default Success Strategy, it's time to leverage the Elevate System coaching tool so you can learn about your own personal Default Success Strategy.

The Elevate System is a key component of transformational leadership. So right now, we're going to do something authors should never do. We're going to tell you to put this book down. Use your device or computer, log in using the following information, and take some time to complete your Elevate profile. It will take only five minutes, and your results will be downloaded to you immediately.

To complete your personalized **Elevate System**™, follow these steps:

- Visit thegreatengagementbook.com
- Click Elevate System.
- Enter this code: **GreatEngagement**
- Follow the instructions.

Once you have your results, read them thoroughly and make notes as you go. Be sure to make note of anything you find revealing or perplexing, and anything you think just doesn't fit you. When you're finished, come back and we'll explain what your profile means.

YOUR ELEVATE PROFILE

Welcome back…and congratulations! We hope you found it useful to complete your Elevate profile, learning what behaviors you're comfortable with, which behaviors make you uncomfortable, and what we've named your "high" and "low" needs. Hang on to your personalized profile; you will want to refer to it in the future.

At this point, you've gained some additional insight into yourself. Perhaps you've done some thinking about your own comfort zone, and your Default Success Strategy. Becoming aware of our unconscious purpose allows us to choose another purpose or strategy. Being aware at this level is the first step in increasing your ability to take more control of your effectiveness. The next step will deepen your understanding of yourself, and begin to help your team members take more control of their effectiveness.

CHAPTER 8

THE COACHING RELATIONSHIP

"A good coach will make his players see what they can be rather than what they are."

—Ara Parseghian

Successful Olympic athletes have coaches. You don't even *get* to the Olympics without a coach. Every great athlete has a coach. A baseball team has batting coaches, pitching coaches, fielding coaches, psychologists who help with mindset, nutritionists, and so on. If we're trying to improve, there are any number of perspectives that can help us…as long as we're open to them.

Most people are reluctant to be coached. We get defensive and protest that there is nothing wrong with us. That's a natural human reaction—an emotional one, not one that we really give thought to. But it's based on a misunderstanding of what an effective coach does. A coach is not someone who addresses remedial issues and solves problems. A coach is someone who can help us unlock potential that we've never accessed before. The difficult part of creating a coaching culture isn't finding someone who can coach us. There are many good coaches. **The challenge is for *us* to become coachable, to listen and learn, not to defend.**

We all have unlimited potential, but we limit it in ways we're not even aware of—and one way is that we all want to prove that we're right. We're afraid of being seen as being wrong. This innate desire to always be right is true of all of us. Notice, right now, how you're probably either strongly agreeing with this or strongly disagreeing with it. (In either case, *you are right*.)

Simply by picking up this book and exploring your Default Success Strategy, you've shown that you can overcome that fear. You're willing to explore what has gotten you this far in life—and to discover how it might be holding you back now.

As we've stated numerous times: your Default Success Strategy works great…until it doesn't.

More often than not, it *is* the perfect strategy for you. After all, you have employed it and achieved great success in your life. It has worked time and again to get you through potentially difficult situations.

In some situations, however, your Default Success Strategy not only doesn't help; it actually works against you. But the chances are that you don't realize this, because you're not aware of using any strategy at all. You think that *you're just doing you*: "This is how I am."

It would be more accurate to say that *your Default Success Strategy is doing you*. It's fashioning an unconscious response aimed at maintaining your comfort rather than striving to achieve your higher purpose.

Our goal is to help people become aware of their Default Success Strategy so they can replace it with more conscious choices when appropriate. The best way to start the process is to go back to your Elevate profile (from the last chapter). Go through it again, this time noting situations in which your style is a strength, and situations where it is a hindrance.

Note that this isn't the same as the usual two-column "Strengths and Weaknesses" routine you're likely familiar with. There are NO weaknesses here. All the qualities you're considering are *strengths*; they are the traits that have brought you this far. This exercise is about examining *in what situations* those strengths are effective, and *in what situations* they are ineffective.

CAROLINE'S CASE STUDY

Consider Caroline, the HR executive from the last chapter who was shocked and upset to find that others saw her as a "cold-hearted witch" (their words, not ours). Caroline's attention to detail brought her rapid promotion, and her thorough research brought her great success in HR. But her Default Success Strategy—thoroughness, attention to detail, and precision—was all based on a fear of being seen as incompetent. She was frightened of being found out.

Caroline's fear made her see the world as black and white, right and wrong, and as a result she was often extremely critical of others. She could be downright dismissive and condescending—which made her team members feel disempowered and diminished. Her higher purpose was to nurture and support others, but her Default Success Strategy was making her act in a way that was diametrically opposite.

We human beings like being right so much that we become addicted to it. Caroline was no exception. She hated being wrong, but she lost sight of the fundamental question any leader should ask themselves: Would I rather be right? Or would I rather be effective?

If, like Caroline, you believe passionately that it is more

important to be right, stop and ask yourself the question in a different way: will this produce the results I'm after?

Remember. As a leader, you can be right one hundred times out of one hundred—and still be ineffective if your team or organization isn't producing results.

Our coaching helped Caroline recognize the forces behind her drive for perfection. Once she understood them better, it was easier for her to see when her Default Success Strategy was useful—and when it was acting against her. She learned to make conscious decisions rather than simply react to situations. She also leveraged her Default Success Strategy by expecting perfection and a better performance from herself as a leader rather than looking down on others when they didn't meet her perfectionistic expectations. This shift has been responsible for her rise from an HR director of a 150-person organization to the CFO of that organization to the COO of a 500-person organization and to her current position, the CEO of a 1,000-person non-profit healthcare organization—all in about a decade.

She's now consciously using her Default Success Strategy only when it works; it's no longer using her.

CONSCIOUSLY SEEKING INPUT

You can learn a lot by working through your Elevate profile on your own. Like an athlete doing drills, however, there are certain things you can't be expected to notice: a failure to listen here, an unconscious dismissive tone there. Try as we might, we can't see everything ourselves.

This is where the value of coaching comes in. Being coachable means being open to others' perceptions of us. It's being open to the idea that ours is not the only reality. Perhaps you know the old "joke" that's not really a joke: What's the difference between reality and perception? Reality is *my* opinion; perception is *someone else's* opinion.

Once Caroline got over the shock of the feedback she received, and her initial defensive reaction, she began to listen. Input from teammates eventually helped her grasp the huge difference between the way she perceived herself and how they perceived her. She came to understand that, if she wanted to be effective with her team members, she'd better learn new approaches.

Caroline learned to ask team members how she was coming across. When she was coming across in a way she did not want, she asked for input on more welcoming ways she might communicate…and be more effective.

Now we're suggesting that you do the same—with team members you trust. We suggest that you invite them to coach you.

When we run workshops, this process happens in the room and, although it has the potential to be messy, it never becomes contentious because we steer people away from criticism, and toward making suggestions for future performance improvement. That said, it does feel difficult. We can only assure you that *the more difficult it feels, the more valuable it's likely to be*. If this exercise is easy, it usually means that either you are not really asking openly or your team members are afraid to be candid.

More likely, as you listen to someone else's view of you, you'll hear things you are uncomfortable hearing. You might be left feeling bruised, like Caroline.

Remember that it's not easy for others, either. Your status within the organization may make it difficult for them to fully express their thoughts about you. One of the burdens of leadership is that your very presence changes the dynamic in a room.

As a starting point, we would suggest that when you ask for coaching, take notes…your job is purely to listen. It's to make it easier for others to say what they feel. You don't have to agree, or disagree; just listen…and feel free to ask clarifying questions. And refrain from trying to explain yourself. It might be uncomfortable, but eventually you'll be better off for it. Simply by listening to those team members, you are turning them into coaches—and that's the first step to empowering them.

AN EXERCISE

Here's how to get started:

- Choose a trusted teammate.
- Have them review your Elevate profile on their own.
- Follow the process laid out on the Coaching Worksheet pages of your Elevate profile.

Note: It is critical that you just listen to your teammate and get their input. If you try to defend yourself or justify yourself, you will shut down genuine feedback, and you'll lose out. Limit yourself to asking clarifying questions or questions to gain more depth.

We recommend going through this exercise with three trusted team members separately. Three is enough people to give you a range of viewpoints, but few enough for you to be able to see a consensus on how others perceive the effectiveness of your strengths.

Listen to what each of your coaches says and take notes on what they identify as your more useful and less useful strengths. You don't have to agree; simply consider their perspective.

Because you are by definition not aware of your unconscious behaviors, receiving input from others is the only way to gain a holistic view of your leadership approach.

Remember: You are going to receive input that disagrees with your own ideas. If you already knew the input, however, it wouldn't be of any value. *The input you most strongly disagree with is the most valuable input of all!*

THE COACH AND THE CRITIC

"The exaggerated esteem in which my life work is held makes me very ill at ease. I feel compelled to think of myself as an involuntary swindler."
—ALBERT EINSTEIN

Coaching is the best way to learn to recognize our Default Success Strategy and make sure we are consciously employing it to help us rather than hinder us. It's a way to overcome the limitations we all put on our success.

If you feel you've plateaued in your pursuit of a higher goal, you're to be congratulated on two fronts. First, you're human, and you're acting in a very human way. Second, you've recognized this plateau and are doing something about it. Most people don't.

The challenge in creating a coaching culture, as we've seen, is that people instinctively defend themselves when they receive input that disagrees with their own opinion. Anyone would. The feedback usually aligns with the criticism from the critic inside their head that is constantly deriding them.

"What critic?" you may ask. We are referring to that voice in our head that has something to say about everything—usually something negative. Our critic has a stream of negative opinions about three things:

- Other people ("They should have canceled the trip because it's raining.")
- Situations ("It shouldn't be raining today.")
- Ourselves ("I'm stupid, I should have brought the umbrella.")

When CEOs are reluctant to accept coaching, it's usually because their internal critic is busy on all three fronts. A CEO might think it useless to accept coaching from anybody else in the organization, because no one else knows what it's like to be in the hot seat (judging *other people*). Even other members of the C-suite, such as the CFO and COO, have never been CEOs, so how could they possibly help? In his former role as a CEO, Tom had several brilliant board members who could have helped coach him, but when he was a new CEO, he felt that turning to them would be a sign of weakness.

Our response to this is simple. Michael Jordan had a coach. Serena Williams had a coach. Are you better at your job than they were at theirs? So go ahead and accept that other senior leaders and board members have something to contribute.

Remember, Michael Jordan's coach couldn't play basketball as well as Michael Jordan; there's no way Serena's coach was as good a tennis player as Serena. They didn't need to be. Your coach doesn't have to be a better CEO than you; they just need to be able to give you a perspective you can listen to and consider before you make decisions. You need to select someone who will be open and give you honest, direct input. This is one of the best ways to become a better CEO.

Next, the critic inside the CEO finds fault with the *situation*, often with a "lack of time." Time is the most precious commodity for leaders. Everyone has a thousand and one pressing issues that need to be decided *right now*, so there's no time for coaching. In fact, there's not even time to read this chapter, so you may just skim past it and move on…

We've seen it all before, and that "lack of time" bubble needs popping. We all have the same twenty-four hours a day, but many leaders struggle to realize that using them effectively is not about time management; it's about priorities. You've already prioritized reading this book because you want to build a transformational culture in your organization.

With all due respect to your schedule, if you really want to take your organization to the next level, you have to make the time.

The final thing your internal critic will undermine, of course, is *you*. It will tell you: "If I accept coaching, I might get found out as being inadequate." Or "Maybe all this openness will cause others to disrespect me…they'll realize I'm controlling, or "I don't like making final decisions," or "I shy away from confrontation." Or "Real leaders never admit to making mistakes."

Guess what? People in your organization already know all about you. **It's just that they're as afraid to acknowledge it as you are to hear it.**

YOUR FIRST COACH IS YOU

Here's another secret about coaching: It's not all about the coach. Coaching doesn't occur when somebody speaks; it happens when someone *listens*. Coaching only helps those who are prepared to be coachable.

Michael Jordan was coachable. Serena Williams was coachable. If you want to be an exceptional leader, you need to be coachable.

Our challenge is this: learn to listen. Think of every scrap of feedback you receive as a gift, even when (or especially when) it smarts. And when your internal critic responds (as it inevitably will) by finding reasons to dismiss that feedback, we strongly suggest that you hush the critic, and embrace the input instead.

We are not suggesting that you always have to agree with the coaching, much less put it into action. We are suggesting that you should *consider* the coaching. Don't dismiss it out of hand. There is always something to be learned from that different perspective. A piece of brain science is useful here: The emotional mind reacts to a situation in hundredths of a second, whereas the executive center of the brain takes up to ten seconds to respond. An immediate reaction to input is an emotional reaction: *Watch out!* We're not saying an emotional reaction is wrong, but it is most certainly defensive. Stop and consider; think through the input. Ask questions to ensure you have a thorough understanding of the other person's perspective.

And be sure to keep the momentum alive by returning to those people for ongoing coaching. This is true leadership by example. Being coachable is one of the first challenges to master in becoming a coach yourself—and that in turn is a first step in instilling a culture of coaching throughout your organization.

SHOULD YOU GO TO THE PROS?

We've discussed your role in coaching your teammates and also how you can involve them in coaching *you*. Both those steps will promote a coaching culture. For quicker, more effective results, however, you may want to hire a professional coach.

We would say that, of course, given that we're longtime professional coaches. However, it's true that many CEOs find turning to a pro highly beneficial.

For starters, professional coaches are outside your corporate structure. You can confide in them things you might hesitate to say even to your most trusted in-house colleagues. In a private, confidential setting, you may feel less vulnerable.

What is more, a professional coach won't be intimidated by your position. Any coach worth their salt has learned to get beyond being intimidated by titles and status.

Finally, hiring a professional coach involves an investment of time and money, so it encourages even the busiest leaders to treat coaching sessions like any other professional commitment. They make time in their day to engage.

Whether you opt for a professional coach for yourself and your leadership team is up to you, of course, but make sure to keep your eye on the end goal, which is to create a coaching culture where everyone helps everyone else to get better, including the CEO.

GOING PRO

If you're going to hire a professional coach, there are two factors that are critical to a successful engagement:

1. Many coaches look for a long-term engagement or job security. Not all see their role as helping you create a coaching culture. If you do decide to hire a pro, look for one that is focused on empowering and teaching you and your people to be good coaches.
2. Most coaches charge for their time. They get paid whether they are effective or not. Look for someone who promises results and is willing to be held accountable.

If you don't hire a pro, enlist your leadership team as coaches for one another. Doing it yourself *can* work. Just putting what you learn from this book into practice will improve things.

Whatever approach you take, from hiring a pro to going it alone, our advice is to empower at least one—and ideally three—people you trust to offer you honest, open, constructive feedback as you undergo your own transformation.

ENGAGE YOUR EXECUTIVE

"All battles are first won or lost in the mind."

—JOAN OF ARC

As we laid out in the Elevate System, the Executive is the counterbalance to the Critic. While your Critic aims to hold you back, your Executive has the power to propel you forward. Your Executive lives, of course, in the executive center of your brain: the prefrontal cortex. This is the character that thinks rationally, learns new things, and knows the right thing to do...and is constantly at odds with Your Critic.

And developing your Executive's ability to keep your Critic in check involves strengthening your Executive's mental muscles. This sounds simple...but it's not. The Critic operates on an unconscious level, like an invisible ninja. How can you fight or control a foe that you can't even see? The skill the Executive needs to develop is to be able to "see"—in other words, become conscious of—how your Critic is influencing you unconsciously.

That's why we recommend working with a coach, because it's the most effective way to develop the necessary muscle. It's also why we use the term *mental fitness*. It's no different than physical exercise: it requires conscious effort and repetition...and it can be uncomfortable.

By working toward your personal transformation, you will spend more time listening to the Executive and questioning your own motives, and less time listening to the Critic. The Executive helps you choose when to utilize your Default Success Strategy and when not to. You take a deep breath, engage your prefrontal cortex, and think through the most appropriate response to a situation.

We call this process "engaging the Executive."

Say you're in a leadership meeting when a department head who seems off their game reports that they have missed *another* deadline. Your Critic might fall back on a Default Success Strategy of dominance and control. It might want to exclaim: "Come on, this is becoming a habit!" The Executive takes a few seconds to consider that response, and recognizes that would be a mistake. It would humiliate the individual and set a bad example for the others in the room. And it wouldn't help you get to the root of the problem of why the leader's performance level has fallen.

ARTFUL COACHING

While we were writing this book, we gathered a group of CEOs we've worked with to present the transformational model we're describing and get feedback. When one of the CEOs made a comment that was somewhat critical, Tom saw a look come over Brad's face. It was a nonverbal response, but Tom could see that Brad disagreed vehemently with the comment. Brad's face betrayed that his Critic was winding up to deliver a defensive response. Just in time, Brad's Executive overrode his Critic, and his response to the CEO was measured and humble—and we profited from some insightful feedback instead of causing friction and discomfort.

Tom had spotted Brad's look, and was pretty sure others in the audience did too. So he turned it into a teachable moment. He described to the audience exactly the process Brad's Critic and Executive had just gone through. It was a great example of both artful coaching and artful listening for the group to witness.

These concepts might sound somewhat fantasy-like, but they are rooted in brain science. These characters, the Critic and the Executive, represent what neuroscience teaches us are two separate parts of the brain. The Critic represents the limbic system, the center of emotion, and the Executive represents our prefrontal cortex or executive mind.

The Critic isn't always wrong. We have emphasized the harmful side of fear because in modern society most danger we fear is imagined: we imagine we might fail, we imagine people might not like us, we imagine we might look silly. Most of these imagined fears never come to fruition. However, our amygdala and the fear it produces are also very useful; without them, we wouldn't get anxious about the big presentation we need to make, or navigating that sticky issue at the upcoming board meeting. In both cases, fear is helpful. That anxiety causes us to think ahead and anticipate what might go wrong; it causes us to rehearse, to prepare. Without this fear, we might go into a situation requiring our best performance without preparing…and risk actual failure.

So we are not saying, "Ignore your Critic." Instead, you should be consciously aware of your Critic's influence. Use your Executive to make a conscious choice about when to empower your Critic's influence and when to ignore it.

THE COACHING CONTRACT

It's probably clear at this point that we are *big* fans of coaching. Huge.

Despite having been professional coaches ourselves for a long time, both of us still have professional coaches of our own.

Hiring a coach, especially for the first time, is an uncomfortable, even intimidating, process. What will you talk about? What will you get out of it? How will you know if the relationship is succeeding?

As with the professional athletes we've mentioned, the coaching relationship must produce winning results, or it's a waste of time. To ensure valuable results, every coaching engagement should be guided by a set of qualitative goals and Key Performance Indicators (KPIs) that are co-created with the client. The client should hold the coach accountable for producing these results in the engagement so they know they're getting their money's worth.

Here's an example of such a set of qualitative goals and KPIs.

QUALITATIVE GOALS

Personal engagement is fostered throughout the organization:

- People in the organization live their mission: a common purpose that is superior to individual agendas.
- People throughout the organization have the authority to make decisions and take initiative to fulfill their responsibilities and produce results.

To create a culture of innovation fueled by personal growth:

- Leaders see their jobs as helping their people grow and use supportive (not punitive) accountability to support personal growth and accomplishment.
- Coaching is the norm in relationships and fosters personal and organizational growth.

A culture of inclusion is advanced and amplifies teamwork:

- Inclusion: people actively invite the contribution and participation of others with diverse backgrounds, lifestyles, and perspectives.
- Departmental "silos" are breached: open communication exists throughout the organization, unimpeded by organizational rank.
- Confronting difficult issues is accepted as necessary to produce forward movement and is conducted in a manner that strengthens interpersonal relationships.

The effectiveness of these qualitative goals will be measured by specific KPIs. Examples:

- Improvement in consumer outcome measures
- Improvement in financial performance
- Increased employee retention
- Increased employee engagement

At the end of each engagement, the coach should meet with the CEO and ask if they received those results. If they say yes, then the conversation can shift to how to continue the work and help cascade it throughout the organization. If they say no, then the conversation should be focused on how to make sure the CEO gets the results they paid for.

We are not suggesting that these are your goals, just that having specific business-based goals is key to an effective coaching engagement. Because we use a team-based approach focused on improving culture, the examples here are very big-picture, long-term qualitative goals. You may have goals that are more focused on your personal development. **What is important is to have a goal-focused relationship with your coach**, whether they are a professional coach or a teammate with whom you are in a coaching relationship.

HARNESS YOUR ENERGY

As we've discussed, true transformation shifts people from fear to love—but fear is a deeply ingrained emotion. People carry around a lot of fear, most of which they're not even aware of. It's below the level of consciousness. It manifests in different ways for different people in different situations; sometimes we're experiencing anxiety, sometimes we're just "uncomfortable," sometimes we get writer's block, sometimes we freeze at the front of the room when we're speaking in public, sometimes we walk away, sometimes we hold our tongue when we want to speak out. Developing the mental fitness to pull yourself out of that emotional state requires more than just committing to a higher purpose. It requires using your Executive to consciously make choices. This sounds simple enough, but...

Humans have been gifted with an amazing mechanism in our unconscious mind: we learn things, and after repeating them over and over, they become unconscious competencies. Examples of this are typing, riding a bicycle, even the use of language itself. Some thought leaders have estimated that it takes hundreds of thousands of unconscious competencies just to drive a car.

Imagine if we had to consciously make every decision involved in driving down the road or even just backing out of the garage. We have to decide to turn the key or push the button to start the car; we have to choose to put our foot on the brake pedal and think about when to move it to the gas pedal. We have to choose to engage the hundreds of muscles within our bodies that are required to push the pedals. We need to consciously choose to listen to each word in the song that's playing on the radio, to look over our right shoulder or our left shoulder when backing out, to look into the car's rear-view camera, and to regulate our heart rate, our respiration rate, and our body temperature while we're doing all of that.

If all those decisions had to be made consciously, life would be impossible. The unconscious mind performs all those functions with minimal effort and with minimal exertion. Our propensity to do all those things on autopilot saves us an enormous amount of energy that would be required if everything had to be thought out.

The task of managing our emotions, as we've laid out, requires us to make conscious choices continuously. That requires far more energy than allowing ourselves to remain unconscious. If we are to perform this job of consciously managing emotions, we must make sure we have enough energy to do so.

We often think about time management, but we rarely think about energy management. Energy management is key to being an effective leader; it is key to avoiding burnout, and it is key to lifelong learning.

Managing energy can be envisioned as a pyramid. At the base of the pyramid is Health. We are not merely referring to health defined as the absence of disease. Take it up a notch to Wellness, the maintenance of oneself to prevent disease, or take it up yet another notch to Fitness, the expansion of one's capability.

There are three aspects of Holistic Health:

The first aspect is physical—selecting the foods we consume based on how they contribute to our fitness, exercising to promote fitness, and sleeping enough to allow for the daily regeneration of our fitness. Attending to all three is the only way to have enough energy and vitality to manage our emotions. When physical fitness diminishes, our energy diminishes with it, as does our ability to think consciously.

The next aspect is mental health or mental fitness. Mental health has quite a stigma in our society, but the fact is that one out of five people suffer from anxiety, depression, or both. Brad has suffered from crippling anxiety and occasional depression throughout his life. He's been to six psychologists, one psychiatrist, and several executive coaches over his career. We tell you this because we think it's important to be open about our need for support in maintaining our own mental fitness. Being open about it is the only way to tear down stigma.

The third aspect is spiritual health or fitness. Do you have a spiritual belief system and a spiritual practice that supports you in life? We are not suggesting any particular religion here, just that spiritual fitness—wherever it comes from—is a huge contributor to anyone's energy. Faith and hope in the future provide energy and sustain humans through the inevitable ups and downs of life.

HOLISTIC APPROACH

Holistic medicine is a form of healing that considers the whole person—body, mind, spirit, and emotions—in the quest for optimal health and wellness. According to the holistic medicine philosophy, one can achieve optimal health by taking ownership and making conscious choices.

The next level of the pyramid is relationships. Even the most introverted people need social contact in their lives, because we are social creatures. Our positive intimate relationships energize us, whether they're many or few. They validate us. They make us feel that we *fit* somewhere, that we are loved and accepted.

The top tier of the pyramid is our higher purpose—which is at the heart of transformation.

This is a foundational point. If we're going to be able to commit ourselves to a higher purpose and behave in a manner that advances that higher purpose, we need to attend to our energy level.

We've depicted this as a pyramid, but it's not a simple structure with cause-and-effect relationships reaching from the bottom to the top. It's more like an ecosystem of co-occurring aspects. Each one can impact the others, no matter where on the pyramid they appear.

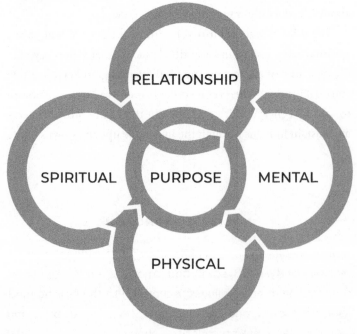

The Energy Ecosystem

Brad, for example, has a tendency to get bogged down with anxiety in the normal course of the work we do. When that happens, he jumps on his bicycle for an hour's high-intensity workout, which dissipates his anxiety and frees up his energy.

Likewise, in periods when business was difficult and depressing, he had a tendency to retreat into himself. He realized about fifteen years ago that he needed to do the opposite. So every time that would happen, he would contact everybody he knew in town to line up lunch or coffee or even just a phone conversation—anything to get connected with people. Getting out and getting connected produced business, though not from the people he was meeting. Instead, the work came because he was consciously managing his emotional state, staying positive and purpose-focused rather than succumbing to the fear of failure, which sapped huge amounts of energy.

We've seen this dynamic in clients, too. We've already mentioned our clients in England who were based in a castle in the English countryside. The team was a bunch of high-tech marketing geniuses who utilized technology to help optimize distribution. They were one of the first entrants into the field and were very advanced. The team was mostly men and a few women, all aged from their late twenties to around forty.

As we spoke, they threw a soccer ball around in the room. After lunch, every day, they would all run out into the huge backyard and kick the ball around for thirty minutes. When they got back to work, you could see the rise in their energy levels and the reduction in their stress.

Running around had exactly the same effect as giving school kids recess. And this tracks with how our brains and body connect because by boosting our physical health, we decrease the likelihood of negative emotions and increase the presence of positive (love-based) emotions. And this attention and discipline then create a virtuous cycle.

THE ENGAGED LIFE INVENTORY

One way to look at this is to use a tool we have developed: the Engaged Life Inventory. It's a tool to help you become more conscious of your level of engagement in the important domains of a rewarding, energizing life.

Simply put, to foster an engaged culture and create an engaged team, we have to have an engaged life ourselves. It starts with how we are doing as a leader. How engaged are we? Remember, we are always leading; our team members are always watching and following our cues.

To use the Engaged Life Inventory, use this link: www.phoenixperform.com/EngagedLifeInventory

IMPORTANT VS. URGENT

We know that when we suggest that you fill in the Engaged life Inventory, your first reaction might well be: "I don't have time for *another* online exercise. I'll skip it and just keep reading the book." To that, we'd urge you to make the time, and we'd explain why with a favorite quote of ours, from Ralph Waldo Emerson:

"The most important things are hardly ever urgent. That is why it is so important to identify what the most important things are and then place them at the center of our lives."

The most important thing to place at the center of your life is...your purpose.

CHAPTER 9

DEVELOPING CONSCIOUS PURPOSE

"What we do for ourselves dies with us. What we do for our community lives long after we are gone."

—Theodore Roosevelt

What is the purpose of your life? How will your world be changed by you having been here?

These are big questions. We're literally asking you what is the meaning of life—of your life?

We're not just talking about a mission statement or the purpose of your organization. We're asking what's the purpose of your *whole* life? What is the overarching purpose that shapes your behavior: as a spouse, as a parent, as a grandparent, a member of your community, and, yes, as a professional in your organization? When we become clear about our purpose, it wakes up with us in the morning. It guides the decisions we make and the actions we take. It becomes the guiding North Star to which we orient everything.

While we work with many CEOs and aspiring CEOs, one of our more inspiring encounters was with a woman who had not a single direct report. A janitor.

Shanice is a custodian at Wayne State University in Detroit, which serves a highly diverse population, with many students from less fortunate backgrounds. In our work with the university, we conducted a workshop to help the participants discern what their purpose was, why they came to work every morning.

It was a challenge to light a fire under most of them—until it came Shanice's turn to speak. Shanice spelled out precisely that she came to work each day to "throw down for the kids." The student body, she pointed out, deserved to be treated with dignity, honor, and respect, since they were the future leaders of the world. Moreover, many of the students had grown up in poverty and were experiencing, for the first time, all the advantages of a top-notch facility. Those students, Shanice continued, deserved a clean, well-maintained environment so they could focus on the studies that would allow them to go on and make the world a better place.

Jaws dropped. The room went silent as her fellow co-workers stared with awe at the janitor. Shanice spent her days mopping floors, cleaning windows, and sanitizing toilets. But she was a true leader. Speaking with passion, she inspired an entire department that day.

Shanice showed up every day in life, not just at work, with a higher purpose. She wasn't there to help herself; she was there to help others. And she had figured that out on her own, long before she met us. She was what George Bernard Shaw called "A force of Nature," one of those people who others would describe as having a fire in their belly—and it was contagious. To be with Shanice was to be inspired by her commitment to serving others. The fact that we met her years ago is a testament to the indelible impression she leaves on everyone she touches.

Most of us need a little help with purpose. We once worked with the owner of several auto dealerships. He was the son of the founder, and he was nagged by the fact that he hadn't founded this successful operation himself. Javier felt that he was riding his dad's coattails, and that he wasn't smart enough or good enough.

Javier's Critic—that nagging, undermining internal voice we met in the Elevate workbook—was working overtime. It just wouldn't shut up. And that Critic was taking a toll, both personally and professionally. On the professional side, while Javier's employees respected his integrity, he was so analytical and uncommunicative that they had trouble relating to him. We helped him realize that his Default Success Strategy™ was all about chasing perfection by removing any room for error. That way, he could never be called out as not being good enough. The result was that he made decisions based purely on cold, data-driven facts and lost sight of the human side of business.

In developing a conscious purpose, Javier came to the realization that he had a deep-seated desire to contribute to the community by improving the lives of both his customers and his team members and their families. He wanted to use his auto dealerships to build relationships and help ensure that all people were treated with respect.

Armed with this new commitment to his purpose, Javier realized that his dry, impersonal style had prevented him from really contributing to his team members and customers. He started to develop his Executive to offset his Critic. He opened up, gave more of himself, and became a generous leader. He built stronger relationships with team members. The entire culture within his dealerships became more open, relaxed, and human as his team members picked up on the new attitude.

Lo and behold, that attitude was transmitted to customers as well—and the company began to sell more and more cars.

As to Javier's personal life, one day he flew off the handle and got angry over a trivial matter. After calming down, he confided in us that he thought he had a drinking problem. He was downing a six-pack of beer every night. But he did more than confess that to us. Having admitted to himself that he had a problem, he gathered his courage and began attending Alcoholics Anonymous meetings regularly. When his drinking ceased, he told us, everything in his personal life improved dramatically—most notably his health and his relationships at home.

Javier didn't set out to improve the bottom line, or become a better father, or a better community member. Once he became clear about his purpose in life, he set out, courageously and consciously, to grow personally beyond his comfort zone, to improve his ability to live that purpose. And the results showed up all around him.

POINT OF VIEW SHIFT

Dozens of times every day, we all make decisions without thinking about the reason we are making them. We just do what's comfortable. They are unconscious choices, shaped by our Default Success Strategy. Decision-making is far more effective if we make conscious choices about how we act, particularly if we focus on other people or a wider context than just ourselves. What is the purpose of our choice? How does it relate to a conscious purpose?

We've already seen that the unconscious purpose that we all wake up with each morning, and that our Critic reminds us about all day long, is self-preservation and survival. It's a deep, primitive, fear-based purpose. It limits us to choices that we know are safe because they have worked for us before.

A conscious choice, on the other hand, helps us develop and become part of a bigger purpose. Remember what George Bernard Shaw called "the true joy in life": *"Being used for a purpose recognized by yourself as a mighty one."*

The mighty purpose Shaw referred to is the inherent human desire to contribute to others. Because just as fear is a primitive instinctive, so too is the desire to help others. We believe passionately that the greatest rewards come when we think beyond ourselves to the greater good.

- *Un*conscious purpose is inner-focused and fear-based.
- *Con*scious purpose focuses on others, is based on a noble desire to be of service to others, and is based in love.

This desire to help others may be at its purest when parents nurture their children. They are willing to show their love completely, even though such transparency risks making them vulnerable. We believe all humans have a similar natural desire to show love to everyone—but it grows stunted over our lives as we get knocked back and hurt by circumstances. We grow a hard shell in order to feel less vulnerable, and inside our brains our amygdala sends out signals that we should stick to our Default Success Strategy in order to survive. Those are the exact same primeval signals that it sent to our distant ancestors when they faced saber-toothed tigers and rampaging mammoths.

All of us have a fundamental desire to help our fellow humans, but as we age, that desire gets covered over with scar tissue from the experiences that wound us. To achieve the true joy of a higher purpose, we have to deal with the scar tissue of adulthood, so let's explore a little more what we mean by scar tissue.

THE BIG PLAN

In his book *Let Your Life Speak*, educator Parker J. Palmer argues that we are all born with a purpose. Palmer says that God gives us purpose as part of His bigger plan. We tend to agree with him, but you don't need to believe in God to accept his argument. Whether you believe in another deity or no deity at all, the idea that we're all born with a purpose is highly attractive—because, otherwise, why are we here?

When we are young, our inner voice is open to living out a higher purpose, but as we grow, that voice is increasingly drowned out by voices from outside. Palmer describes those outside voices as a collection of *shoulds*. You *should* make a lot of money. You *should* drive a nice car. You *should* live in this sort of house. You *should* seek out this sort of spouse.

Unwittingly, those voices get taken up by our inner Critic. We end up orienting our actions toward satisfying everyone else, trying to look good to others, trying to prove that we are worthy. These motivations shape our daily actions. They become part of our unconscious purpose.

ONE MAN'S JOURNEY

Brad is a living example of the way our pure, childlike grasp of our purpose in life can be trampled by experience—and of the way we can get it back.

As a child, Brad used to play a game with his friends, pretending they were all garbage men. They would climb on the bumper of his mom's car and toss his toys up onto the trunk, pretending they were throwing garbage. Hanging off the back of a garbage truck going fast along the street while clearing the trash looked like a great adventure. He actually wanted to be a garbage man when he grew up. It looked like a great way to help others, and he would get to ride the back of the truck and take home all that great stuff he found!

But then around the age of ten, his friends began to shift their focus to who had the coolest baseball glove, the greatest bicycle. When Brad went to his dad to ask for these things, his dad instead offered him the lawnmower to use to earn money. So began a lawn business. By age fifteen, he was mowing up to ten lawns per week, making big money.

Brad's success in making money made him feel like he fit in (he was a terrible athlete and not a good student), and it became the source of his self-confidence. In fact, he continued the business through college, expanding to house painting and handyman services. By that time, he was investing in the stock market…and it was all about the money.

At the same time, in high school, Brad became a sounding board for many friends, particularly girls with dating problems. One girl confided to him that she was contemplating suicide. She told Brad in confidence, but after much internal agonizing about what to do, Brad decided he had to tell her parents. He did, and they got their daughter into counseling that probably saved her life—but at the cost of a friendship. The girl didn't speak to him for thirty years, until they reconnected at a high-school reunion.

Looking back, it seems clear that Brad's purpose was to listen to and help others. He had the gift of empathy and insight into what drove people, and was someone people felt comfortable talking to. Like all of us, however, he was surrounded by outside voices full of *shoulds*. Brad's father was a successful businessman. They lived in a nice part of town. Brad wanted to live up to his father's expectations.

By this stage, Brad believed that his purpose—in as much as he had one—was to make lots of money, to have a nice home in a nice part of town, and everything that went with that.

The result: upon graduating from college, Brad declared his goal was to become a millionaire by age thirty.

He spent his twenties working toward that goal. He made more money than any of his friends, had a beautiful home, a beautiful wife, and won sales awards—he was living the "American Dream!" At the same time, though, he hated his job and was depressed. He began smoking two packs of cigarettes a day, and three-martini lunches became the norm. Then, when he was twenty-nine, his first child was born. His wife had quit working ahead of giving birth to their daughter, so they had lost her income. Meanwhile, Brad had invested money in the business, cutting his own income. When he filled out his tax return for the year, he noticed their income was down about forty percent from the previous year.

It was a huge blow to his financial ambitions, yet he asked himself, "Are we any less happy than we were last year?" *The answer was no.* In fact, now that they had a young baby, life seemed more gratifying than ever.

Brad realized that happiness had little to do with their financial situation. In concentrating on how much he could earn, he'd been pursuing ends that he didn't really care about at all. They had nothing to do with his true purpose in life. He wanted to be a sympathetic ear, someone to help others with life's challenging times, a loving father, someone who could be counted on for help.

We've already described how Brad went to some personal transformation workshops and then got invited to *coach* some workshops…and he realized that *this* was his life's calling. He wanted to help others. Brad sold his business and began training to become an executive coach. On the face of it, that made no sense for someone who had only been focused on money. But if you looked deep enough into his past, at the purpose that shone through before those other voices kicked in—the purpose Brad believes God gave him—to go on an adventure, helping people, well, it made perfect sense.

The story also underlines that the process of generating a conscious purpose for your life isn't just about making something up or writing a statement. It's a declaration of—and a commitment to—a future that might be very different from whatever present you are currently living.

THE DAVID INSIDE YOU

There is a passionate leader inside all of us. We know this to be true. As we saw earlier, the Renaissance artist Michelangelo believed that the figures he sculpted already resided inside the blocks of marble he carved. His job was to chip away at the marble to reveal what was hidden within.

There is a leader within *you*, driven by a higher purpose. The process laid out in this book will allow you to reveal that leader, in all his or her glory. You can chip away those superfluous *shoulds*. **When we overcome our unacknowledged fears, we become a conduit through which the power of a higher purpose—perhaps God-given—finds expression.**

CLARIFYING YOUR PURPOSE

While it's important to define and explore the concept of conscious purpose, we know that some of you are already familiar with yours. If that describes you, congratulations!

For decades, we've worked with nonprofit CEOs, healthcare CEOs, and school system Superintendents who came to us with a good understanding of their purpose. Their field of work was clear evidence that they had chosen to help others. In most cases, they had turned down more lucrative career opportunities to do so.

When we ask these leaders to describe their purpose, however, many struggle. Worse yet, many recite their mission statement. Their purpose is clearly there, but it often seems to be hazy or vague, as if covered by a foot and a half of water. In those cases, we help them better understand their sense of purpose. To become a truly transformational leader, it's not enough to *have* a sense of purpose. We have to be able to *articulate* it, to share it with others, to use it to inspire and evoke a sense of purpose in them.

Consider one of the great leaders of the twentieth century, the Reverend Doctor Martin Luther King Jr. His commitment to, and work toward, equality was outstanding in its own right. But it was King's ability to articulate his purpose that inspired a nation. His ability to inspire lay in his oratory:

I have a dream that one day on the red hills of Georgia, sons of former slaves and sons of former slave owners will be able to sit down together at the table of brotherhood...I have a dream that my four little children will one day live in a nation where they will not be judged by the color of their skin but by the content of their character...

Notice how Dr. King speaks in word-pictures. You can see those children and you can see white and black people sitting at a table on red hills. This is the hallmark of great leadership and why leaders are referred to as *visionary*. Their ability to speak in word-pictures automatically generates a picture in the listener's imagination. This is what evokes the emotional response we refer to as inspiration or excitement, and what motivates individuals and unifies teams toward a higher purpose.

While Dr. King is a hero of ours, and one of the twentieth century's great orators, leadership takes many forms...and so does articulating your purpose. All CEOs must overcome a fear of public speaking, but it's not all about look-at-me leadership. There are many people who lead effectively with a relatively quiet, behind-the-scenes style.

One who comes to mind is Sarah, a self-described introvert who's happiest curled up with a good book. Despite her lack of outward zeal, Sarah is the brilliant CEO of a nonprofit organization of more than 1,000 employees. She'd been with the organization for years when we began working with her team, but our workshop helped them each gain clarity on their individual purpose. Not surprisingly, Sarah's purpose is to help those less fortunate share in the abundance of our economy by empowering them to develop.

Some of the best leaders, including Sarah, lead from behind. Rather than dragging people along with them, their commitment is to inspire others to move forward. Sarah came to understand that, while it was fine for her to be an introvert, it was also important that she lead people to share the same burning purpose she felt. This realization has allowed her to grow the organization and better serve its clients.

HIGHER LOVE

"The best way to find yourself is to lose yourself in the service of others."
—GANDHI

The idea of a higher purpose rooted in love is an ancient one. The ancient Greeks recognized several different kinds of love, including *philia*, or brotherly love, and *eros*, or erotic love (self-explanatory!). In the Greeks' eyes, the highest form of love was *agape*. Agape is defined as a willful, sacrificial love that takes delight in helping others. It was memorably described by M. Scott Peck (author of *The Road Less Traveled*) as the extension of oneself for the growth or benefit of another. This highest form of love, in which we put others before ourselves, serves as a foundational premise in several of the world's major religions, including Christianity (the word *agape* appears widely in early Greek translations of the Bible). It is a form of ancient wisdom that has taken hold in myriad cultures around the world across thousands of years. Earlier, we suggested that Jesus was perhaps history's greatest transformational leader. He changed the world from an "eye for an eye" mindset of revenge to one rooted in forgiveness, reconciliation, and love: "Love your enemies, do good to those who hate you, bless those who curse you, pray for those who mistreat you" (Luke 6:27–28). His is a story of putting others first and making courageous choices, including the ultimate sacrifice of dying for others.

If you are a Christian, our hope—and goal—is to help you grow closer to God by modeling His love. If you follow another faith or none, we believe that the higher purpose of helping others is universal and that anyone can benefit from realizing this truth.

COURAGEOUS HEART

The word *coeur* is French for "heart," which is the root of the English word *courage*. We love this term because just as the heart pumps blood through our bodies, keeping us alive, so courage is more than just another virtue: it is the heart of virtue. It brings the other virtues to life and enables us to live by them. Without courage, you cannot be strong or humble.

It takes courage to speak our mind when we know we'll run into opposition. It takes courage to refuse to listen to our Critic. As a CEO or a leader, we have to make many decisions every single day—and each one demands courage. We'll need to place the needs of others above our own desires, and fears. We need to do what's right for them, and for the organization and its stakeholders, rather than just for ourselves. Above all, it takes courage to commit to a higher purpose, and to go public with it. Our Critic will try to convince us that it is corny, or idealistic, or that people will laugh at us or scorn us.

True leadership requires this combination: commitment to a higher purpose and the courage to enroll others in that purpose. It's also our *job!*

LEAP OF FAITH

"Faith is taking the first step even when you don't see the whole staircase."

—MARTIN LUTHER KING, JR.

This chapter has been building toward a key moment in your transformational journey: declaring your purpose. This will require courage because most of us aren't accustomed to hearing this type of talk in a work setting. It's a huge leap of faith simply identifying our purpose. To then go and share it with other people is hugely courageous.

Discussing our purpose can make people uncomfortable. As a society, we don't tend to talk about it much in case we are judged negatively. Our Critic tries to anticipate what others will think, or say: *Who are you to come off so high and mighty that you have a purpose? Purpose, schmurpose—we're just trying to make widgets here. What are you, some kind of crazy idealist?* The voices our Critic anticipates are exactly the ones we mentioned earlier in the chapter. They want to push us back to our Default Success Strategy; they don't want us to be encouraged by a higher purpose, to step outside our comfort zone.

When we explore purpose, we pair people so that they learn about one another and can co-create each other's purpose. They share and encourage one another, get inspired by one another. Then we have each person share what they talked about with their partner with the entire team, and they all get inspired—and they all realize that they share a common commitment to being of service. We create an atmosphere in which talking about high ideals and purpose is normalized, not weird. People see that others get inspired and energized by these conversations, and that **shifts their relationships from seeing one another as their personality, or their Default Success Strategy, to seeing one another as their higher purpose.** It becomes the foundation for a whole new level of partnership within the team.

REDISCOVERY

Committing to your higher purpose will have effects throughout your life. Maya ran a nonprofit healthcare organization, and she worked long hours because she felt that she had to do everything herself. She had to look after her team members, which meant that she had to protect them from being overworked. So she took on more work herself. It was all part of her Default Success Strategy. She was so busy that she was gasping for survival; she once told us, "I have to get out of here to survive."

Maya realized that her purpose was actually to help other people develop and grow—and that her behavior was actually *thwarting* the growth of her team members. She wasn't letting them grow through the productive pressure of work. So she set out to replace her unconscious purpose with her conscious one...and people stepped up and took on more work. They learned new abilities and increased their capacities, and they were grateful for the opportunity to learn and grow. That not only gave Maya a sense of accomplishment, but also freed up her time for other things.

A few months later, Maya had another breakthrough. She had been married for seven years, and she and her husband had had some problems. But now she felt that she was more present for her husband, and more available to him. Their marriage was in a much better place. They were talking about moving and rekindling their relationship by starting afresh. She was bringing her conscious purpose to her marriage.

George, a buttoned-up banker in his mid-sixties, spent most of his life listening to his Critic and letting other voices define him. Throughout his long career, he had played by the rules. He dressed the part, joined clubs, and played a lot of golf. He kept his head down and fit in. And it had made him pretty successful. The challenge was that as he compounded his money, he also compounded regret.

Along the way, George had drifted away from his wife. He'd been so busy with his career that he'd lost touch with his family.

George realized that in discovering his purpose, he had some work to do at home. He went home, sat on the edge of the bed, and began to ask his wife the same questions that had helped him learn his purpose. The pair spoke for hours in a way they hadn't for many years. The conversation ended with both the husband and wife in tears as they cleared away the barriers that had gone up between them. He was in tears again as he recalled the story.

Both of those marriages evolved from transactional to transformational, from fear based to love based, because someone committed to their higher purpose.

THE PURPOSE OF PURPOSE

While many would argue that purpose is its own reward—recent academic studies have also discovered some objective benefits to having a higher purpose. Vic Strecher, a University of Michigan professor and author, has researched the topic extensively. His book *Life on Purpose* reported the results of a study of 7,000 middle-aged American adults.

Dr. Strecher and his team followed the individuals for seven years, and rated them on a 7-point Scale of Purpose, ranging from "lacking all purpose" to "entirely motivated by purpose." Their findings included the following statistics:

- People with heart disease reduced their risk of dying by 12 percent merely by increasing their purpose score 1 point.
- A 1-point boost on the scale reduced the risk of heart attack by 27 percent.
- Seniors with a low score on the scale were over two times more likely to develop Alzheimer's Disease than were those closer to the top.

Moreover, when people with a commitment to a higher purpose come together to form an organization, great things happen. That is the cornerstone of this book—and our own purpose! In *Firms of Endearment*, author David B. Wolfe compared companies with a social purpose against the broader Standard & Poor's 500. Over a fifteen-year period, the socially engaged companies (what Wolfe calls "firms of endearment") showed a return on investment of 1,681 percent, compared to a 118 percent return for the S&P. That's right—a factor of ten and change.

A clear purpose is the basis of any successful for-profit or non-profit organization. Show us an organization whose team members are clear about and committed to their purpose of providing value to others, and we'll show you a successful organization. By contrast, show us an organization that is about survival or just making money, and we'll show you an organization in decline.

PURPOSE PAYS

One of the last K-Mart stores in the country was in Metro Detroit. If you walked into the store, you would see team members who ignored their customers in favor of restocking shelves or whatever other task they were focused on. K-Mart's management had been focusing on regaining the success they enjoyed in previous decades, on making money, and on simply surviving. The employees were inattentive. As a result, you could shoot a cannon through the parking lot without hitting a car.

When this K-Mart inevitably closed, a store called Meijer moved in. They did a facelift, but when you walked into this store, you were greeted by friendly employees who wanted to know if you needed help finding something. If you did want something, they would walk you to the location where you could find it. Even the cashiers were friendly and interested in you as a customer. They sold the same products that K-Mart did, even most of the same brands, but now Meijer's parking lot was gridlocked with people and cars. The store is still enjoying enormous success.

It pays to have a purpose that all employees are individually committed to.

EVERYONE IS A LEADER

Cast your mind back to Shanice, the janitor whose story opened this chapter. Shanice was living proof that, if you find purpose in your work, you will create better outcomes. Her story reminds us of another involving President John F. Kennedy. JFK was being led on a VIP tour of a NASA facility early in the Space Race, after the president had announced the program to send humans to the Moon. Spotting a young man working a push broom, the president went off-script, as he often did, and began to chat with him. When JFK asked what the other man was doing, the janitor proudly replied, "I'm helping to put a man on the Moon, sir."

As a leader, it is your job to ensure that every employee, regardless of their job function, is clear about their purpose.

Ensuring that each employee is clear about their personal purpose is very different from the conventional approach of "Let's write a mission statement." Memorizing a mission statement doesn't give people any real sense of meaning, excitement, or inspiration.

People committing individually to a purpose they find personally compelling, on the other hand, gets them out of bed in the morning. It serves as a source of energy and power for them personally and for the team collectively. *This* **is your job as a leader: to evoke personal commitment to a higher purpose.**

TWO EXERCISES

We suggest this is a good time to complete the following two exercises: a core values exercise and a personal purpose exercise.

We suggest that you partner up with someone, perhaps one of the people that you're getting coached by. This could be your spouse, a friend, or a colleague from work. Each person would do the written exercises separately. And then get together, share your answers, and talk through them. You can each act as a coach for the other by interviewing each other. Help one another get clear about your thinking.

First, take some time to complete the following core values exercise:

Personal Core Values Exercise

Step 1: From the list of core values on the next page, place a check mark next to approximately twenty values most important to you.

Step 2: From the list of core values checked, circle the ten most important values.

Step 3: Complete the following sentence:

The three personal core values most important to me are...

CORE VALUES (FEEL FREE TO ADD ANY ADDITIONAL VALUES.)

___ Accountability
___ Achievement
___ Action
___ Advancement and promotion
___ Adventure
___ Affection
___ Arts
___ Caring
___ Challenging problems
___ Change and variety
___ Charity
___ Close relationships
___ Community
___ Compassion
___ Competence
___ Competition
___ Conformity
___ Cooperation
___ Country
___ Creativity
___ Decisiveness
___ Democracy
___ Ecological awareness
___ Economic security
___ Efficiency
___ Ethical practice
___ Excellence
___ Excitement
___ Expertise
___ Faith
___ Fame
___ Fast living
___ Fast-paced work
___ Fidelity
___ Financial gain
___ Freedom
___ Friendships
___ Growth
___ Having a family
___ Health
___ Helping other people
___ Helping society
___ Honesty
___ Independence
___ Influencing others
___ Inner harmony
___ Integrity
___ Intellectual status

___ Involvement
___ Job tranquility
___ Knowledge
___ Leadership
___ Location
___ Love
___ Loyalty
___ Market position
___ Meaningful work
___ Merit
___ Money
___ Nature
___ Order
___ Personal development
___ Physical challenge
___ Pleasure
___ Power and authority
___ Privacy
___ Public service
___ Purity
___ Quality of what I take part in
___ Quality relationships
___ Recognition
___ Religion
___ Reputation
___ Responsibility
___ Security
___ Self-respect
___ Serenity
___ Service to others
___ Sophistication
___ Spirituality
___ Stability
___ Status
___ Supervising others
___ Time freedom
___ Trust
___ Truth
___ Wealth
___ Wisdom
___ Work under pressure
___ Work with others
___ Working alone

Additional values (add your own):

___

___

___

___

Personal Purpose Development Exercise

Being clear about your purpose will make it easier to talk about it with people, and sharing your purpose is the best way to get people thinking about theirs.

The second exercise includes five questions we suggest you use to begin work on your Personal Purpose. Take some time to consider them. Find an area that is comfortable and secure, relax, and clear away the concerns and thoughts of the day. This exercise is designed to stimulate your thoughts and feelings regarding personal hopes, dreams, and commitments for the future. *It is not an assessment of your past.* There are no right or wrong answers. Let your thoughts freely consider each question, and write down your thoughts.

1. What led you to your career and/or has kept you in it?

....

....

....

....

2. What do you consider to be your true accomplishments in life—the things that make you proud, make you smile?

....

....

....

....

3. What impact or legacy do you want to create with your life?

....

....

....

....

4. If you knew you had only five years left to live, what would you want to accomplish?

....

....

....

....

5. After having lived a full life, how do you want your eulogy to read?

....

....

....

....

As part of the exercise, imagine also that you're writing a book about your life that will end with your death. What sort of book would it be? If you got to read the book in the afterlife, what would you think of the main character? Did he or she accomplish much that you admire? Does their story inspire you? This isn't an exercise that's original to us, but it's a useful way to consider what life you are authoring for yourself. Think about what you could change to make the story a more uplifting book—and then change it in your real life. Remember: you are the author of your life, and you can't change the story once you're dead!

Follow-Up

When you're ready, we suggest you and the person you are discussing this with reconvene to talk through your answers. This will not only clarify your thoughts, but help you connect with them emotionally. Explaining your answers and receiving positive feedback (as we know you will) can be very self-affirming. It will help you muster the courage to share your purpose with others. This, in turn, will help you develop a culture of sharing in your organization.

Your Personal Purpose

Having completed both the values and purpose exercises, what common threads do you see in the two? You may want to simply list bullet points, or you may feel able to begin to create a statement about your personal purpose in life.

Don't rush to write a statement! We're not pressuring you to come up with it right now; for many people, it's better to let ideas simmer awhile. Also, you don't have to be a perfect wordsmith, although many people have a tendency to try. Instead, rough out some sort of statement to remind you of your purpose so that you can talk about it with people. Rather than simply reading a statement, you can talk about what it means to you, talk about how it applies to the situation you're in, or paint word pictures that illustrate it.

Here are a few examples of such reminders as food for thought:

A statement:

My personal purpose is to help people realize and grow toward their divine potential.

Or...a list of discussion points:

- To help people see their God-given potential
- To support people in growing toward their potential
- To enable economic and social opportunity for all

Or...a visual reminder:

Tom uses this picture of Mount Sneffels, Colorado, as a reminder of his commitment to help people grow spiritually toward God. The inspirational beauty of the mountain evokes the same emotion he feels from seeing someone grow spiritually.

ENGAGEMENT

"Engagement" is a popular topic of discussion in leadership circles. Team members, especially younger team members, want more than to merely turn out widgets—even if the widgets are excellent and the work is lucrative. Today, team members want to feel genuine engagement with their work and employer. As we laid out at the start of the book, Engagement is the antidote to the Great Resignation.

As a result of this new interest, it's easy to find surveys on the *symptoms* of engagement. That's all well and good, but it doesn't go far enough. Purpose is the *root cause* of engagement. When people understand their personal purpose and its connection to our professional life, we engage in the organization's mission, and we engage with others to accomplish that mission. We adopt the corporate mission as our own, becoming highly effective team members and true ambassadors of the company.

That's what makes great organizations. And it's why great organizations have leaders who focus every day on creating more engagement. Perhaps it's worth considering a change in your title from Chief Executive Officer to Chief *Engagement* Officer?

MISSION STATEMENTS

When we ask most people about their purpose at work, they start to fumble with their phone to find their mission statement online. For us, that illustrates the problem with mission statements. If people have to look them up, the mission isn't living *within* them. Mission statements are often lofty pronouncements that give a 30,000-foot view of the whole organization, so they don't relate to people at different levels. They are inert. They don't stir people's passions or engage their hearts.

Your job as an inspirational leader is to constantly help define people's purpose within the broader purpose, bringing personal meaning to *all* levels of the organization. It's about what Simon Sinek calls the "why?" *Why* are we doing this? Find the meaningful answer to that question, and it will transform how people see their jobs, turning the most mundane of jobs into meaningful work.

A great leader is not an extraordinary person. It's an ordinary person with an extraordinary purpose.

CHAPTER 10

THE TRANSFORMATIONAL CHOICE

"I am not what happened to me, I am what I choose to become."

—Carl Jung

Alex embodies a transformational leader. As a Chief Technology Officer, he is, like many in the tech field, quite introverted: quiet, self-critical, analytical. By his own admission, he's not at all comfortable in a public-speaking role.

Nevertheless, Alex volunteered to lead a segment of our Transformational Leadership Experience workshop. His subject was dialogue—the value of really listening to and learning from team members—and he stood up in front of an audience of forty colleagues and was absolutely brilliant. He made his points by re-creating his own inner dialogue and explaining how his own inner voice often prevented him from listening to others. He not only told the story, he acted it out. It was extremely funny and, more importantly, extremely effective. The whole room hung on his every word.

We've been in business for thirty years, and this was something special. We marveled at his performance. Afterward, this shy CTO admitted he'd been very nervous before the event. But once he got up, his nerves were replaced by a desire to help his colleagues grow and improve. He went through a transformation from being motivated by his unconscious purpose, avoiding fear, to being motivated by helping the people in the room grow so they could better serve their elderly clients. He didn't just talk about transformational leadership; rather, he was an example of *being* a transformational leader.

Sometimes, transformation is as simple as asking yourself: *Will I allow my fears to rule me? Or will I base my behavior on my higher purpose?*

We face these decisions ourselves, even after decades of explaining fear and purpose to others. Most days, we can't wait to get to work. Other times, though, we balk. We tell ourselves we're tired, or under the weather, or overworked. In reality, we're simply scared. Perhaps we're nervous about potential negative outcomes, perhaps we anticipate problems or confrontations—for sure, our unconscious mind is looking to avoid risk.

That's when we need to remind ourselves of our higher purpose: helping our clients grow so they can better focus on helping *their* clients, who can then in turn help still more people. **The cascading effect of this positive change improves the lives of thousands of people and is the purpose that displaces our fears in times of trouble.**

THE LEAP

A few years ago, Tom's wife, Jessica, got an idea that she says just "wouldn't leave her alone." With decades of experience helping the uber-wealthy manage their finances, she couldn't understand why the same insights and tools available to multimillionaires weren't easily accessible to non-millionaires. Simply put, she wanted to change the financial futures for millions of people by leveraging the power of a financial planning app. The app she envisioned would be aimed at Gen X, Millennials, and Gen Z.

The app, Pocketnest, would enter the crowded FinTech marketplace. Like all startup founders, Jessica knew that the statistics weren't exactly on her side: 90 percent of startups fail in the first twelve months; only 2 percent of all venture capital goes to women-led startups; and Pocketnest would be in the Midwest, not in Silicon Valley. And the elephant in the room: she would be going up against the titans of two powerful industries: finance and tech.

Jessica persevered, making the tough decision to leave a great job and a steady paycheck. She didn't have a team, a foolproof plan, or deep pockets—but she did have a passionate commitment to her purpose.

Well, here we are a few years later, and Jessica has built a team of twenty, raised various rounds of venture capital, and is ready to present to some of those financial industry giants in the quest for the next round of funding. The team aspires to improve the financial futures for millions of people, and Pocketnest is well on the way, with over half a billion dollars in assets being tracked.

And they are just getting started!

FROM PROBLEMS TO PURPOSE

Most people who attain positions of leadership are excellent problem-solvers. That's a wonderful thing, but we've found that high-performing problem-solvers share an unfortunate trait: The instant Problem A is solved, their mind immediately moves on to Problem B. Then C, then D, and so on. By the time they get to the end of the alphabet, there's a new Problem A.

Sound familiar? If this describes you, the problem is that you never stop to acknowledge anything you accomplish along the way, and you probably treat your employees the same way. **Racing from problem to problem, without stopping to reflect on what's been accomplished, provides no sense of fulfillment.** It's like running all day on a hamster wheel...running hard and getting nowhere. It is worse than not being motivational; it's *de*motivational. Everyone keeps running all the time, and the inevitable outcome is burnout.

Try taking a conscious gratitude break, both as a leader and for yourself.

It's hard for CEOs to take a moment to consider their successes and those of their team, but it's vital. Understanding your purpose helps, because it allows you to appreciate the impact all your hard work has on others. And, paradoxically, slowing down like this actually helps you accomplish more, faster, because you are taking time to inspire your people so they are energized and able to better serve your customers.

For example, health centers came under immense pressure after COVID-19 struck. They were on the front lines, vaccinating tens of thousands of people in tents in parking lots and scrambling to administer new and innovative treatments like monoclonal antibody treatments. Frustration and burnout ran high. Naturally, health staff were at high risk of getting sick. Many people quit, including top doctors. Team shortages followed, making the job even tougher for those who did show up.

During one of our meetings with a health center, the burnout within the team was obvious. We started asking a few questions to help team members reframe. We asked how many folks their center had vaccinated since the pandemic hit. The answer was *about 60,000*. Then we asked, "What impact do you think that had on their lives?"

The room was quiet for a minute. Finally, someone noted that the people they'd vaccinated had been able to return to work and support their families. Next, the CEO pointed out that many of their clients lived in poverty and lacked the essentials that most of us take for granted. She raised the example of a young mother who lived in a remote area and had no car. For a week, she had been unable to get diapers and food for her young children. Because of lockdowns, none of the woman's friends had been able to step in to help as they usually did. Feeling isolated, powerless, and depressed, the young mother confessed on the phone with a health center team member that she was seriously contemplating doing something unthinkable to her children and herself.

The CEO continued that the team member who had taken this call immediately hopped in her car, raced to the store for diapers and groceries, and delivered them to the struggling family. She followed up by connecting them to social services that would continue the care. The team member had saved three lives.

When the CEO finished, you should have seen the faces in that room as everyone realized that this was just one story out of hundreds. They had all saved lives. They all made a difference.

By harkening back to their purpose, the team members transformed from an exhausted, burned-out group to one full of pride, ready to take on the next challenge. One of the managers in the room actually said that the story reenergized her to focus on such accomplishments with her team. But that will require her to make a series of small but critically important choices: stay on the hamster wheel...*or* pause to celebrate?

WRITE IT DOWN!

Want to improve your organization quickly without spending a dime? **Start by saying "thank you" more often.**

Here's a more specific way of saying thank you; it's an assignment to help put the wind back in your own sails—and those of your team members—and help counteract burnout. First thing in the morning, every morning, write down one success achieved by a team member the previous day. Then announce it to everyone, celebrating the success. For extra credit, take a few minutes to handwrite and deliver a note of thanks to that employee or manager. Nothing fancy, just a quick thank-you for the contribution.

A simple habit like this will make you more aware of and grateful for the valuable contributions all team members make. It will give you, and them, a few minutes away from the intense what-problem-needs-solving-next hamster wheel and help everyone transition from a critical-problem orientation to a grateful, goal-oriented orientation. You will become an inspiring leader rather than a tactical manager.

Earlier in the book, we explored the topic of building mental fitness. Just as you develop your muscles by exercising, you can consciously improve your mental fitness. This gratitude habit is a great example. Just as you must commit to regular gym visits if you want to see results, it's important to commit to writing down a success *every workday* in order to make it a habit and reap the full benefits.

In this era of intense pressure, intentional focus on the purpose that inspires you is more important, and more difficult to achieve, than ever. We're all constantly being buzzed, pinged, and dinged!

Slowing down and stepping off the wheel requires a conscious act of will.

Exceptional leaders do just this. They consciously choose to slow down and inspire their people by acknowledging progress. And a simple and sincere thank-you is one of the most powerful tools there is.

Who will you inspire today?

CHOOSE YOUR PURPOSE

Transformation is as simple as making a conscious, intentional choice between your personal purpose *or* your unconscious purpose, your Default Success Strategy. It's a process of ongoing, moment-by-moment choices.

Do I:

- Correct my team member because I know they're going to make a mistake *or* support their growth by letting them learn from their mistake?
- Ignore that my team member isn't getting the job done, to make them comfortable *or* support them by acknowledging the failure and coaching them?
- Take charge and insist that the issue be addressed my way *or* empower my team members to do it their way?
- Express my anger and frustration with my team member *or* have a supportive coaching conversation that causes them to take responsibility for shortcomings?

Creating a transformational culture and being a transformational leader requires these kinds of conscious moment-by-moment choices. On one hand, it's that simple; on the other hand, it's that difficult.

Oh, and it's 7:00 a.m. on a Sunday morning, and I just made a conscious choice: keep working on this book *or* have a cup of coffee with my wife?

Coffee it is.

And here's a choice for you: Am I going to put this book down when I'm done reading and go on to the next thing *or* choose my higher purpose and engage my team to take our effectiveness to a whole new level?

What conscious choice will you make *right now*?

If you choose to engage your team, read on. We have lots of specific methods for you to try.

CHAPTER 11

ENGAGE!

"The signs of outstanding leadership appear primarily among the followers."

—MAX DE PREE

So far, this book has been about you preparing yourself personally as a leader. The work we've asked you to do has been like going to the gym to get in shape to be ready to play the game. Now turning that potential into reality requires daily action to engage your team members.

If you're disappointed with your people, look in the mirror. Your primary job as a CEO is to foster a personal commitment in every employee to serving their customers. This defines engagement. Having people on your team who lack that commitment is like a professional football team with players that don't like football but hang around for the paycheck. Firing someone because they lack commitment is a failure of leadership, but it happens sometimes. As a CEO, it's your primary job to engage them so that they love football again. Your secondary job is to empower them with the agency to deliver on their commitment.

The capstone project is putting everything you have learned to work throughout your team. You've started at the core, declaring your own purpose, so your team is next. As you work your way toward impacting every employee, your job is to inspire every single team member, whether that's two people or 20,000. You achieve that by enrolling people around you to take on the organization's purpose as their own so they internalize it and allow it to guide their actions.

LOVE THY NEIGHBOR

Building a transformational purpose in your organization doesn't come from declaring values and hiring consultants. Rather, it arises when you as a leader talk about your personal purpose and use it as the North Star for the day-to-day decisions that steer the destiny of your organization.

Eli, the CEO of a healthcare organization, is deeply religious; and when we met him, he was very clear on his personal purpose: caring for others, or in other words, Matthew 22:39: "*Love thy neighbor as thyself.*"

Eli's purpose meant that he abhorred the way our society often warehouses our seniors. It inspired him to make the seniors living in the company's facilities feel like respected, engaged members of society. He was doing everything in his power to make his company an exception and to serve as a model for the industry.

He was an inspiring leader, loved by all. However, he tended to avoid conflict, which meant, counterintuitively, that he wasn't always easy to work with. Ducking difficult conversations meant he wasn't always clear about the organization's direction. At least he recognized this, so he approached us to help spread his personal purpose throughout his seven-member leadership team. He wanted to engage them in his purpose so that they could further spread it across the entire organization. Each of those seven individuals had a transformative experience, but there's one in particular we want to tell you about.

She was the company's HR director, and we'll call her Serena. Serena came to understand that her unconscious purpose—linked to her Default Success Strategy—was to protect the organization from being sued. Her fear-driven self was terrified about potential litigation caused by improperly documenting poor work performance.

Protecting the organization was an entirely laudable aim, but Serena realized that she had taken it too far. She had grown so focused on discipline and documentation that she had become, in her own words, the Discipline Police. This realization came to her as a result of feedback she received.

When Serena said this out loud in a room with the CEO and her leadership peers, we could see the heads start to nod. Everybody was very well aware that she was the Discipline Cop.

Because of her reputation, Serena realized that anytime she entered a room, employees looked at their shoes, convinced she was about to fire somebody.

This insight was terribly upsetting, but Serena came to understand her higher purpose. It certainly wasn't to strike fear into her colleagues' hearts. Instead, she wanted to help human beings grow and develop. If you were to ask her, in simple terms, she would want her team—and her family, friends, and neighbors—to feel like she loves them and is committed to their growth and betterment. She wanted to put the *human* back into *human resources*.

When Serena figured this out and explained it, the senior leaders were blown away. People throughout the leadership team began to come to her for her coaching and support.

Serena rewrote her job description from scratch. It's now all about coaching and inspiring so that employees at all levels can better serve customers. In fact, Serena enrolled in a rigorous coach training program and has polished her coaching skills to serve her newfound purpose.

TRANSFORMATIONAL TOOLS

We've seen Serena's story repeated by others thousands of times. Her successful transformation is the result of a comprehensive set of tools exceptional leaders employ. To be effective, one can't just *lead*. Effective leaders must also *manage* and *coach*.

Each of these sets of tools performs a different function and addresses a different aspect of transformation. Being clear about the distinction between leadership, management, and coaching allows you to choose when to use each one, in the same way a carpenter knows when to use a saw or a hammer or a screwdriver; they are three separate tools for three separate functions, and you need them all to build a house.

Up to this point in the book, we've addressed leadership exclusively. That's because leadership is the power source, the fuel of any organization. It creates the **aspiration** in the formula for engagement:

$$\text{Engagement} = \text{Aspiration} + \text{Empowerment}$$

Management and **coaching** are additional tools to be used to create empowerment. You can use them to equip people with the necessary permissions, awareness, responsibility, and capabilities they need to engage their best selves in their personal aspiration. But leadership comes first.

Leadership, management, and coaching are a *set of tools* rather than roles within your organization. Whether you call yourself a leader or a manager or a coach, you need to use all three of these tools.

- An effective leader uses leadership, management, and coaching.
- An effective manager uses management, leadership, and coaching.
- An effective coach uses coaching, leadership, and management.

The distinction between your title and the use of these tools is crucial. That's especially true in today's environment where other thought leaders tend to denigrate management and say things like *"Be a leader, not a manager"* or *"Be a coach, not a manager."* That approach ignores the absolute necessity for managing in addition to leading and coaching.

DEFINITIONS

Let's start with a conceptual definition of each of the three tools. (We stress that we are not offering the single *correct* definitions—you may define them differently. We are offering a very pragmatic way to view each of these tools that allows you to focus your actions and to target specific behaviors.)

It takes courage to lead.

LEADERSHIP

- Leadership is generating a vision for the future that people adopt as *their* future—it becomes *their* aspiration. Such a vision changes people's focus from an unconscious, fear-based purpose of self-protection to a consciously generated, love-based purpose of contributing to the growth or benefit of others.
- Use leadership to inspire team members to move beyond behaving in ways that are driven only by their habitual, automatic behaviors.
- The trend to write mission statements or engage in values conversations is an attempt to inspire people, but true leadership isn't about writing statements. Statements or slogans don't inspire.
- Leadership connects people personally to a love-based higher purpose. Using leadership effectively engenders commitment within people, creating aspiration in others.
- Leadership also helps people become aware, understand, and accept the current reality as it is.

COACHING

Coaching is about supporting people's personal growth. Transformational coaching helps people to realize when the vicious cycle is kicking in: they're on unconscious autopilot, their Default Success Strategy is steering them, and their fear-based behaviors are thwarting their own progress. Transformational coaching is focused on helping people improve their mental fitness by developing their Executive muscles.

MANAGEMENT

Management is about creating explicit agreements and promises—not mere expectations—for actions or results. Management is what creates cultures of integrity, where people can be counted on to do what they say they'll do. Management assures that people have the authority to fulfill their promises and replaces blame with supportive accountability.

ONE, TWO, THREE

Take a minute and think about how much of a typical week you spend on leading, managing, or coaching? As an example, when Tom first became a CEO, he was spending about 10 percent of his time leading, 10 percent on coaching, and 80 percent on managing.

Leading: _____ Managing: _____ Coaching: _____

The first step should always be leadership. It comes before management and coaching. In this role, the leader's task is to create a unifying and compelling vision in each team member's imagination so that each team member then has their own aspiration. The leader makes sure that everyone is aligned on where they are now, and uses the power of inspirational purpose to generate commitment.

Leadership is utilized to create aspiration, while management and coaching are utilized to empower people. Leadership sets the vision; the next step, management, turns it into action. The mission and goals will only be achieved if people commit to achieving results or tasks, and the role of management is to create a structure of accountability and integrity. This transition to action is the backbone of effective execution, and is produced step by step, promise by promise. People are willing to make promises and be held to account because they are committed to the mission and goals. And they must be empowered, given the authority to make the decisions necessary to produce the results they have committed to.

The third step is coaching, which creates a culture of support. In order for your organization to move from the current reality toward the future state, each individual must grow beyond their Default Success Strategy. They have made commitments and promises that require behaviors or knowledge beyond their current capabilities, so they need to be able to ask for support—and that support must be readily available. Coaching also involves training and learning to help people grow in order to fulfill their promises.

The conscious and skillful application of leadership, management, and coaching together produce a culture of inspiration, accountability, and personal growth, and an organization that produces breakthrough results. As a leader, it's your challenge to develop a conscious awareness of when each set of tools is needed, and the skill to apply them.

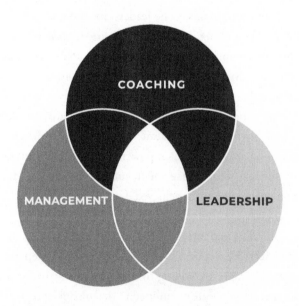

PUTTING IT ALL TOGETHER: AN EXAMPLE

We've defined leadership, management, and coaching as three separate sets of tools. That is accurate, but they work in combination—and when combined, they're very powerful.

One day several years ago, a friend of ours mentioned that she had been to Weight Watchers. Brad asked innocently, "What do they do there?" and she explained it to him. It occurred to Brad that Weight Watchers uses the combination of leadership, management, and coaching very creatively. In fact, it's their business model for helping people change deeply ingrained behaviors.

The first thing Weight Watchers does is run advertisements on television. Those ads don't say "If you're overweight, come and see us" or "Being overweight is unhealthy, and you should address it." Instead, they say nothing about being overweight. They simply show Jennifer Hudson, who has a whole new physique from what we had previously seen, dancing on screen, being energetic, excited, and very alive. Or they show grandparents or parents on the playground, playing with their kids. Both those are examples of healthy, active lifestyles. If you're at home sitting on the sofa with a soda pop and a donut, thinking, *Wow, I wish I could be that energetic and active,*" and you get inspired to change, then they've just done a great job of leading you by giving you a picture of the future that could be yours. *That's the leadership piece.*

When you join Weight Watchers, the first thing they do is ask you how much weight you want to lose in the next week. You say, "I want to lose one pound." They then ask you if you will commit to losing one pound, and they gain your promise. *That's the management piece.* They talk with you about how you might change your diet this week and what kind of activity or exercise you might engage in. *That's the coaching piece.*

When you come back the next week, they have you step on the scale. They do an accounting or support you in being accountable for whether you lost the pound and simply acknowledge whether you did or didn't lose it. Again, that's the management piece.

If you lost the pound, they give you an "attaboy" and provide more coaching about how you might continue your success with diet and exercise. If you didn't lose the pound, they talk with you about why you want to lose the weight, how it will benefit you and others (the leadership piece again), and provide more coaching to help you succeed in the next week.

Leading, managing, and coaching help people change their most deeply ingrained behaviors. Weight Watchers is an internationally renowned organization whose purpose is to foster behavioral change, and its model is essentially to lead, manage, and coach people. That is a testimony to the effectiveness of these three simple concepts. Think of the millions of people Weight Watchers has helped change their behavior over more than half a century.

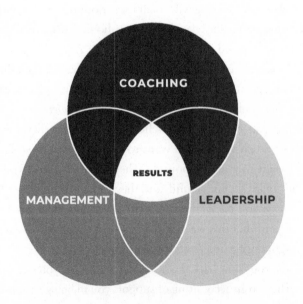

IMPLEMENTING CHANGE

Leadership, management, and coaching are the tools you can use to engage with your team members. These sets of tools each require very different behaviors, and we have yet to meet anyone whose Default Success Strategy makes all three a natural fit for them. In other words, you will find that at least one of these, or maybe two, are outside your comfort zone. When Tom first became a CEO, a good day for him was having his office door shut so he could "crank out" some work. Luckily, he soon realized that his job was no longer to get work done but to lead, manage, and coach the potential and greatness of his team.

In the chapters that follow, we will outline specific methods and behaviors you can engage in to implement them. We can't stress enough that employing a coach, either a colleague or a professional, to help you implement these uncomfortable behaviors is critical.

CHAPTER 12

LEADERSHIP: SPREADING THE PURPOSE

"There is only one way under high heaven to get anybody to do anything... And that is by making the other person want to do it."

—DALE CARNEGIE

Every great organization has a clear purpose at its heart. This is worth repeating over and over again because it is absolutely essential and oftentimes missing. And one cause of the "Great Resignation" that followed the COVID-19 pandemic was a lack of purpose, a lack of aspiration in the work. Many people decided to quit jobs that weren't meaningful and that they had been putting up with for years. The "Great Engagement" will occur because you as a leader do a great job engaging people in your purpose. You might be familiar with engagement surveys based on measures such as "Do you have a friend at work?," "Do you like your manager?," or "Is your manager supportive?," but true engagement

LEADERSHIP IS GENERATING A
VISION FOR THE FUTURE THAT
PEOPLE ADOPT AS THEIR FUTURE—
IT BECOMES THEIR ASPIRATION.
SUCH A VISION CHANGES PEOPLE'S
FOCUS FROM AN UNCONSCIOUS,
FEAR-BASED PURPOSE OF SELF-
PROTECTION TO A CONSCIOUSLY
GENERATED, LOVE-BASED PURPOSE
OF CONTRIBUTING TO THE
GROWTH OR BENEFIT OF OTHERS.

comes from engaging people in a purpose they find meaningful and that compels them to engage in new behaviors. So your first job in creating the Great Engagement is to imbue your leadership team with purpose.

The human mind or memory is temporal. Things pass in and out of our consciousness quickly, so we constantly revert to our unconscious habits or competencies. Your job as a leader is to keep presenting higher purpose to your team members until it becomes ingrained in their unconscious minds. The purpose comes from their heart, and their heart recognizes it, so it has true meaning for them personally.

This purpose enables Transformational Leadership to occur because it helps every person to transform their mindset from the automatic fear reaction to a love-based response. This focuses primarily on transforming three of the personal and cultural mindsets we introduced in Chapter 3:

- **Personal agendas** are replaced by **personal commitment** to an aspirational mission.
- **Assuming nefarious intent** is replaced by **assuming positive intent**: leadership aligns people's intent so that we interpret other people's words or actions in a constructive or optimistic way.
- **Drama** is replaced by **radical acceptance**: rather than complaining about conditions, we embrace them so we can figure out how to respond to them. If we are to change the current reality or conditions, we must first accept things as they are.

A PURPOSE-DRIVEN ORGANIZATION

Once you and your team members identify your personal purpose, you may want to systematically connect people's personal purpose to their role in the organization. Look at how pervasive purpose is in your organization. We're going to suggest a framework or mental model to use to think about this, albeit a fairly superficial treatment of a subject that we spend hours discussing with clients.

Humans are creatures of habit who become stuck in our methods—but people who cling to yesterday's methods become obsolete. People who maintain a rigorous focus on their purpose are willing to continually change their methods and approach in order to accomplish it. What inspires such creativity or innovation in any endeavor is a clear purpose or end result.

An organization is a group of people organized to accomplish the same core purpose. That core purpose breaks down into many more that are usually made up of sub-purposes that define a department's purpose, each team, and ultimately each person's purpose within each department. Their progress toward that purpose is measured by key performance indicators (KPIs), which are usually time dependent.

- Your **core purpose** (also known as your mission) is a description of the value or benefit you are committed to providing to the key stakeholders that you are devoted to serving. It is the reason you exist. It provides a qualitative target that provides a future state to which the people of the organization are committed. When the term Mission is used, people automatically think of a Mission Statement, which, as we have stated, has no power to inspire. We are talking here about evoking a purpose from each person that they aspire to.
- A **sub-purpose** is a qualitative description of each of the component parts required to achieve the core purpose. Sub-purposes are organized into tiers: first tier, second tier, third tier, and so on. Ultimately and ideally, every position in the organization is defined by a sub-purpose that links it directly and clearly to the core purpose.

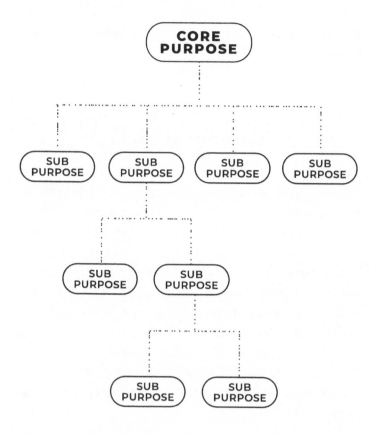

Once you have identified the core purpose and sub-purposes, it's your job to inspire leaders to continue the process of identifying sub-purposes so that they eventually apply to each job description within the organization. In that way, every person in the organization is clear about his or her purpose and how it rolls up to the overall purpose of the organization.

Identifying the core purpose and sub-purposes is not a once and done, however. A leader's role is to continually renew the core purpose and sub-purposes for themselves and their teams so that they become indelibly imprinted in individuals' minds.

In this way, the organization structure becomes a reminder

for each person of what their inspiring part of the organization's mission is.

EFFECTIVE MESSAGES

There are close parallels between leadership and advertising: both set out to encourage people to make certain decisions. An advertiser's job is to indelibly imprint a product on the minds of their potential consumers. An ad is effective when the majority of the population knows it by heart and are so sick of it they don't want to listen to it anymore. Advertisers know that repetition ingrains the message in the neural pathways of people's brains. A leader's job in an organization is to repeat, reframe, and recontextualize the purpose so it becomes ingrained and team members take it on as their own. You may have noticed we repeated a few key concepts in this book for this same reason—**to help you engrain it into your brain**.

RECEIVABLES AND SELF-RESPECT

Recently, an organization asked us to conduct our Empowering Management workshops with their executive team. The workshops' aim was to provide a venue for leaders to declare the purpose and sub-purposes of each team member's position, with KPIs we'll get to shortly. They are a fifteen-site federally-qualified health center that provides primary care to patients who are on Medicaid or have no insurance. Mary, the CFO, emerged from the workshops, having declared that her purpose was to partner with each site manager to ensure their site was financially viable, and that patient dignity was enhanced.

The piece about dignity was particularly important to Mary. For some time, she had been upset by the number of patients who didn't pay their bills and went to collection. But Mary's issue was not what you might think from a CFO. She didn't care about the company getting paid—but she knew that sending someone living in poverty out for collection on yet another bill was very disempowering and was detrimental to their self-image and their health. Mary realized that the breakdown was occurring at the front desk of the organization. The team members at the desk were not explaining to patients when they admitted them that they could name their own price. *People will pay if they name their own price.* They also will emerge with a sense of dignity and respect.

Mary's purpose added an element of genuine inspiration for her and the members of her billing and collections team that links them directly to the organization's mission—directly contributing to their patients' mental health—rather than viewing their job as the mundane act of sending out bills and collecting money.

Adding measures such as KPIs to this kind of purpose gives meaning to the numbers. Now, when Mary does a receivables aging report, it means something to her and her team, and inspires action.

Mary not only discovered her own higher purpose. She also figured out the best way to spread it throughout the organization by showing her team members how they were individually contributing to the organization's purpose in a way that allowed them all to aspire to their own higher purpose. But to achieve that level of leadership, a CEO has to start with themselves and their purpose: they have to choose to transform themselves before they can help others transform.

PRACTICES FOR EFFECTIVE LEADERSHIP

As you prepare to imbue your team with a greater sense of purpose, there are some proven methods we'd like to share. We have used them and seen clients use them over the years to effectively keep purpose alive in people's conscious minds. This is not, by any means, an exhaustive list; be creative—come up with your own ideas.

Share, Share, Share

Talk about your purpose at every opportunity. In a discussion about a project the organization is engaged in, start by talking about how the project relates to your purpose. In a discussion reviewing the status of an initiative, start by talking about how the initiative advances the purpose of the organization. In *every meeting*, take a moment to connect what's being discussed to the purpose of the organization.

Write Up a Statement That Articulates Your Purpose and That of Your Company

This is not a PR "mission statement" exercise. Create a statement that comes from your heart. Frame it and put it up in your office, and use it in your email signature. Display it in places where people will see it and ask you about it. Talk to them about it. Explain what it does for you and about how it animates you in your job. Help them relate to it as they think about their job with customers, other employees, and other stakeholders.

Talk about the Organization's Mission Statement

Have a "mission moment" at every meeting; point out to team members accomplishments that are examples of your mission in action. This makes people realize that it is real, not just an empty statement. They can see the results of it in action—but only if they are pointed out.

Ask Them Questions

Get them thinking about the purpose and making the connections for themselves. Do this one-on-one and in meetings:

"*What does our mission mean to you?*"

"*If we were using our purpose as a guide, what decision would we make here?*"

"*How does this opportunity serve our purpose...or not?*"

"*If we use our mission as the guide, how might we address this situation?*"

Put It in Writing

In written addresses or newsletters to your team, frame every accomplishment, every initiative, every action, every customer story, every employee story in the context of your purpose.

With Your Team, Develop an Inspirational Sub-Purpose for Each Department

Have them do it with their own teams. Have them post and talk about how the daily tasks and routines advance that goal.

Stop Delegating

Yes, you read that right. Delegating is about the needs of the person doing the delegating: the definition of delegate is "to send or appoint a person as your deputy or representative." That's giving people work that *you* want done. The person being delegated *to* can oftentimes feel dumped upon. Effective leadership flips this 180 degrees. **Leadership creates the desire in people to do the work: if someone wants to do something, then they are excited to do it. (That's true empowerment.)**

Have Frank Discussions about the Current State of Affairs

Help people understand, become aware, and accept things as they are. Don't candy-coat things.

Acknowledge People for Their Daily Contributions to the Mission and Goals

Caring is a competitive advantage. When he became a CEO, Tom started a practice of sending several thank-you notes each and every week to employees, partners, and vendors who did something to advance the purpose of the organization. It might have been a teacher helping a student with reading, a guidance counselor helping a student apply for college, an HR specialist doing a great job of serving an employee, or a vendor taking extra time to teach students something about their profession. At one all-employee meeting, the CEO acknowledged each person who served meals to the children. You would have thought it was a football game by how loud the cheers and claps were for each and every individual.

It doesn't matter how big or small the accomplishment. What makes an impact is taking the time to thank people for contributing to the purpose. That keeps the purpose alive in their minds and makes people feel appreciated for committing to that purpose.

Celebrate Progress

The Critic, who we met in Chapter 8, makes our brains like Velcro for negative experiences, which the Critic clings to, and Teflon for positive experiences, which just slide right by. Exceptional leaders counteract this by taking the time, constantly, to celebrate successes and forward progress.

It is only when this seminal job of *Leadership* is done that you can move on to *Management*. Leadership must *always* precede management.

CHAPTER 13

MANAGEMENT: A CULTURE OF INTEGRITY

"Honor your commitments with integrity."

—Les Brown

Management focuses primarily on transforming these mindsets from the list we saw in Chapter 3:

- **Powerlessness** is replaced by **authority** that is proportionate to responsibility.
- **Incongruence** is replaced by **integrity**: we do what we say we're going to do.
- **Blame** is replaced by **personal responsibility and supportive accountability**: we don't ask "Who is to blame?" but "How am I responsible for fixing or changing this? And how can I use supportive accountability to help others?"

The essential function of management is to *empower* people by creating a culture of integrity. What does it mean to have integrity? The root of the word is the same as the root of the word *integrate*. *Integrity* means to integrate two things: your word and your actions. In our usage, it really is that simple. Integrity is doing what you say you're going to do—and this definition does not include any moral or ethical judgment of what you "should" do.

A culture of integrity is therefore a culture where people count on one another to say what they will do and then do what they say. The key to that is accountability, which is the act of keeping track of whether we keep our word or not and acknowledging so. An organization with a culture of integrity is a powerful social group. Integrity is the backbone of organizational success.

Management is the structure of explicit agreements that define what each person promises to be accountable to produce. Your job when you're managing is to make requests of team members to gain their promise to either accomplish results or do a task, then follow up with them to see if it was done, celebrating success and acknowledging failure—without judgment or retribution. This simple act of gaining people's promise or their word and supporting them to do what they say they're going to do is the source of integrity in any organization.

Management systems keep an accounting, or score, of what people are accomplishing. There are many project management programs or dashboard programs that can be extremely useful tools. However, in most cases, they end up passively tracking failure or success because the interpersonal aspect of management is missing. There are no specific promises and follow-up from managers to ensure accountability. Without promises between people, these systems are like weather-tracking systems: we watch the results happen, but we have no real ability to impact them.

Management needs quantifiers such as KPIs—or OKRs (Objectives and Key Results) or metrics—to eliminate the confusion of interpretation.

EFFECTIVE MANAGEMENT: GET A PROMISE

"The key to growth is to learn to make promises and to keep them."
—STEPHEN R. COVEY

There is a step-by-step transactional method to effective interpersonal management, and it all begins by making a simple request. This may sound elementary, but only a very small number of people are adept at asking people for what they want or need.

A good request is:

Direct: It comes from me to you: "I ask that you..."

Specific: It outlines the specifications that define successful accomplishment: "...deliver a report outlining the year-to-date sales through the 15th of the month..."

Has a time frame: "...by December 20th at 5:00 p.m."

There are two possible responses to such a request. Either people agree and they give you their promise, or they decline. That's it, although when people decline, they may make a counter-offer.

The idea that people have permission to decline a request sticks in the craw of many of our clients. They say things like, "It's their job. How can they say no?"

The fact of the matter is that people need the ability to manage their own word. This is one way to empower people. If people *don't* have the authority to manage their word, they *can* have no integrity. To put it a different way, if you can't say *no*, then you can't say *yes* with any integrity.

In many cases, managers simply tell team members their

ONE CAN NOT MANAGE PEOPLE.
ONE CAN ONLY SUPPORT PEOPLE
IN BEING SUCCESSFUL BY SECURING
AGREEMENTS AND PROMISES.

expectations without securing an explicit agreement or promise, and as they walk away, the receiver of the expectations thinks to themselves, *I can't possibly do that. I have too many other things I've already promised. Oh well, hopefully they won't notice.*

The manager thinks they've got it covered and won't find out until the due date that there's a problem. If, instead, they had given permission to the person to say no, they would know well ahead of time that they have a problem and would either have the opportunity to work out whatever the conflict might be or have an opportunity to coach the person in how they might get it all done.

RESOURCES AND BARRIERS

Not only do people need the permission to say no to operate with integrity, they also need to be able to ask for the resources they need in order to say yes. They may need permission for overtime for their department personnel, they may need new equipment or software...they may need something from another department that they have not been getting in the past. The list of possible requirements is endless. When presented with the cost of doing what has been requested, you may actually see that the result you have requested is not worth the investment, and dial the request down.

The process of getting a commitment from both the requester and the promiser can surface barriers that are impeding progress. Sometimes, major longstanding breakdowns between departments are surfaced and get resolved, paving the way to dramatically improved performance. Only by pressing for a promise will you discover all the potential resources needed and barriers to resolve to get what you are requesting.

Perhaps the most important resource is **authority**. When someone promises to produce a result, do they have the authority to make the decisions necessary to get the job done? This is one of the factors managers are least aware of, and one that produces great resignation if not granted. To be given the responsibility for an outcome without the authority is to be destined to fail before one even starts. Granting explicit authority is one of the most significant ingredients to empowerment. It tells others that you trust them enough to give them *power* to decide. This point was made best by William McKnight, chairman of the board at 3M, in 1949. His philosophy has been credited as the source of the company's success and reputation as an innovator:

> As our business grows, it becomes increasingly necessary to delegate responsibility and to encourage men and women to exercise their initiative. This requires considerable tolerance. Those men and women, to whom we delegate authority and responsibility, if they are good people, are going to want to do their jobs in their own way.
>
> Mistakes will be made. But if a person is essentially right, the mistakes he or she makes are not as serious in the long run as the mistakes management will make if it undertakes to tell those in authority exactly how they must do their jobs.
>
> Management that is destructively critical when mistakes are made kills initiative. And it's essential that we have many people with initiative if we are to continue to grow.

A BROKEN WORD

We all break our word sometimes. If you're not breaking your word sometimes, then you're likely making safe, comfortable predictions, not promises. In other words, you're promising things that will happen anyway, not things that will stretch you. You *will* break your word—so how can you keep your integrity when that happens? Treating your word as your bond means that, as soon as you see you're not going to be able to keep your word, you let the person to whom you gave your word know so that a new promise can be negotiated, a new way to accomplish the task can be developed, or other tasks might be rescheduled. This is honoring your word.

It's interesting to look at the language. If I give my word to you, you now have my word. If you have my word and I'm going to break it, then I need to come to you to clean it up.

BAD REPUTATION

In recent years, as it has become apparent that leadership and coaching are vital to an organization's success, management has received a bad reputation. Our LinkedIn feeds, which include a few threads about leadership, are full of articles that say things like "Don't be a manager, be a leader" or "Don't manage people, coach people." Those kinds of mantras reflect an overly simplistic point of view. They ignore the fact that, **without measures, and without people making promises to advance the purpose of the organization, very little progress can be made...and what progress *is* made is not coordinated.** Management is a vital function that must be performed in any organization.

That doesn't mean management requires the same commitment of time as leadership and coaching. It takes little time to make requests and gain promises. It takes very little time to simply review with someone how they performed against their promises. As a CEO, we would suggest that leadership probably occupies 35 percent of your time and coaching 50 percent, leaving maybe 15 percent of your time for management. However, it is a vital 15 percent. Those leaders who consciously spend their time accordingly produce the most exceptional results.

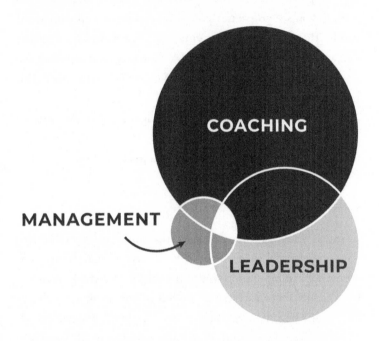

SUPPORTIVE ACCOUNTABILITY

Some of the most common complaints we hear when we work in organizations are about a lack of accountability. Leaders say, "If only people around here were more accountable for results." Meanwhile, the people who work for them gripe, "Managers don't hold people accountable here."

Everyone understands that accountability is a key ingredient to the success of any organization, so why does it seem so rare? A large part of the answer lies in the widespread misunderstanding of what *accountability* means. It's often equated with blame when things go wrong: "Someone needs to be held accountable" really means that someone needs to be fired. That sort of accountability is threatening and counterproductive. It leads to demeaning feedback that undermines people's sense of pride in their work. Recent studies show that performance reviews that focus principally on blame for performance problems demotivate people and cause productivity to suffer for months. (No wonder some team members dread reviews and many managers avoid doing them.)

Another cause of the absence of accountability is that people tend to think that it applies to others rather than to themselves. Accountability often seems to be something that *others* lack. It's rare that someone thinks *they* are lacking in accountability. We all say yes to lots of things without writing them down or tracking whether we followed through or not. We agree to do things and don't follow through simply because we forgot, and are oblivious to the fact that we broke our word.

For a more productive definition of accountability, we need to look at the origin of the word. Its root lies in the word *account*, and *accountability* means nothing more than keeping an account of results produced compared to results *promised*. In work settings, it is a basic statement of actual performance compared to promised performance, based on clearly agreed upon KPIs that measure a person's effectiveness in their job.

This creates a black-and-white account with no judgment attached. Most likely, the person is succeeding in some areas and failing in others, as is the case for virtually everyone. In this accounting, it is important to celebrate successes as well as address failures. In fact, we think that celebrating success is more important. People's own Critic will cause them to amplify and focus on their failures, so as a leader, you need to help them stay focused on their successes too. If you don't, they probably won't, either. Success breeds success.

This objective review of the promises a person has made is the basis for a coaching discussion to produce a plan to improve performance. This accounting might be reinforced by a system of rewards (for better than promised performance) and consequences (for worse than promised performance), but rewards and consequences alone will not bring about accountability.

We emphasize the word *promised* here because empowering people with accountability involves supporting them in accomplishing things that advance their aspirational purpose, supporting them in accomplishing things that they have voluntarily committed to because they aspire to the purpose. Without their aspiration and their promise, we are simply exerting our will on them, telling them what to do and when to do it.

When leadership engenders an aspirational purpose within people (**remember, leadership must *always* precede management**), those people will embrace being accountable for results. Effective management then becomes a natural support for each person to attain their commitment. They want to make good the promise because the result is important to them, and they know that having someone support them in being accountable supports their personal success. Managing this way is empowering!

Implicit expectations that people accomplish results and holding them accountable for what they haven't promised is disempowering and leads to resignation. Gaining someone's voluntary promise to produce and supporting them in being accountable is empowering.

A STORY OF INTEGRITY

One of our clients is a nonprofit provider of primary care services with fifteen sites and about a thousand employees. One of the challenges they faced was that they lost 2 percent of their revenues each year for the previous five years. They could afford this because they had a significant endowment, but they realized they needed to operate more sustainably. We engaged with them for about a two-year period and worked with the executive team and middle-management team through the process we've outlined in this book. One of the decisions they made was that, rather than try to manage profitability centrally, they would create a culture of integrity where each person was accountable for producing results. The leaders worked with all their site managers to develop KPIs that measured the health outcomes of their patients and the profitability of each site.

In the course of their work with us, the CEO and executive team realized that they had been making all the decisions for years, while complaining about their management teams' performance and being judgmental about their capabilities. They began to engage with one another and their teams and begin to lead, manage and coach, thereby empowering their teams. Rather than judging and complaining about their team members, they inspired them to want to make promises for better patient outcomes and better financial performance, and they got site managers and managers throughout the company to make specific promises for specific KPIs.

Within one year, the organization turned the 2 percent deficit into a 1 percent surplus. For a Medicaid-financed nonprofit, a 3-percent swing is quite a dramatic improvement. Even more impressive, at the same time, they improved their patient outcomes so significantly that they won awards. The creative implementation of supportive accountability produced extraordinary results.

PRACTICES FOR EFFECTIVE MANAGEMENT

We have seen this list of practices used to create a culture of integrity over the years. This list is not exhaustive by any means, however. Be creative—come up with your ideas.

1. **Be rigorous about your personal integrity.** In all things, do what you say you will do. When you "give" your word, honor the agreement.
2. **Be on time—or early—for all meetings as a demonstration of integrity.**
3. **Make requests of people.** Gain their promise—but make sure they have permission to say *No.*
4. **Follow up with people to support them in honoring their promises to you.** Doing so before a deadline provides a friendly and supportive reminder that builds a collaborative relationship. Doing so after the deadline lets people know you are paying attention and care about supporting them.
5. **Use a personal management system** such as Outlook Tasks or Google Tasks to keep track of both:
    A. The promises you make to others
    B. The promises others make to you
6. **Recognize people for good performance** at the time it happens.
7. **Recognize people for poor performance** at the time it happens.
8. **Create Key Performance Indicators (KPIs) for every person's inspirational sub-purpose.** Be sure to make them stretch targets, not easy-to-obtain targets. Review them with people regularly.
9. **Create a dashboard** of the most important KPIs.
10. **Meet regularly to review the dashboard.** This is a fantastic way to generate supportive coaching.

CHAPTER 14

COACHING: THE ULTIMATE COMPETITIVE ADVANTAGE

"Everyone deserves a champion…who insists that they become the best that they can possibly be."

—RITA PIERSON

If *leadership* is generating a view of the purpose that others take on as their own and *management* is creating explicit agreements, then what is *coaching*?

Simply put, coaching is empowering; it is supporting people in keeping their word. That support can take the form of training, encouragement, feedback, and helping people see how their Default Success Strategy is getting in the way of effective performance in their job…or helping people see how their Default Success Strategy is a huge asset in the performance of their job.

There are three types of coaching:

1. **Tactical:** Tactical coaching could take the form of training, giving people specific methods to accomplish tasks, or telling people how to do something. It is the simplest and probably most often used form of coaching.
2. **Developmental:** Developmental coaching is focused not on telling people what to do but on helping them develop their own approach and their own capability. Developmental coaching is designed to help people increase their skills and increase their mastery of content.
3. **Transformational:** Transformational coaching is the type of coaching we've been discussing in this book, helping people shift from behaviors that make them comfortable to behaviors that advance their purpose. Effective transformational coaching helps people to become aware when fear is motivating them and to stop and choose.

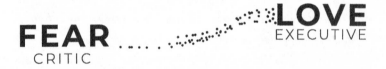

Coaching focuses primarily on transforming this collection of the personal and cultural mindsets we saw in Chapter 3:

*   **Fixed mindset** shifts to a **growth mindset**: we realize that we and others are capable of growing our intelligence, behavior, and even attributes of our personality.
*   **Judgmentalism** is replaced by **elevation**: rather than judging others as weak, incapable, or uncommitted, we assume they

are resourceful and look to lift them up and help them be more effective.

- **Exclusion** is replaced by **inclusion**: we accept others who disagree with us or who come from significantly different backgrounds or cultures.
- **Retribution** is replaced by **psychological safety**: we contribute to others' growth or benefit by letting them express themselves and deliberately creating an environment where they feel free to speak up.
- **Conventionality** is replaced by **creativity**: we take the risk of trying new things because we are more committed to our organization's purpose than we are to being safe.
- **Gossip and avoidance** are replaced by **active resolution**: if we have issues, we put them on the table and talk about them to resolve them.

All types of coaching have one key in common that distinguishes coaching from nagging, cajoling, and know-it-all ism:

Coaching is only coaching if it's asked for!

In other words, people have to be willing to listen. If people aren't open to coaching, if they're not in a position to receive input, they will not receive it. If we accept the premise that coaching is only coaching if it's asked for, then our first job as leaders is to get people to ask. It sounds simple enough, but take a moment and think about how many of your staff are actually open and receptive to input or feedback. How many *know* they are right and are stuck in their opinion? How many feel threatened by feedback, especially since you're the boss?

Asking for coaching always feels vulnerable. We've been brought up in a society where "knowledge is power." Asking for coaching is to admit that you don't know, or that you don't have the capability. We have all been trained since we were young that this is a bad thing, and our Critic—that voice in our head—doesn't want us to admit it. And this unconscious force is significantly holding back the potential of you and your team… and thus the results your organization can produce.

UNLEASHING POTENTIAL

What interpersonal factors must be present for someone to ask us for coaching?

First and foremost, people need to know that we are on their side. They need to know that we are committed to their success. Only then will they genuinely open up and ask us for our input. If people think that we're coaching them only to advance our own success or to make us look good, they won't open up. That's not a compelling enough reason for them to be vulnerable. There are other factors, but this is the big one. Think about it. Would you hire a coach that you didn't trust was truly committed to helping you, no matter how knowledgeable or how well-known?

COACHING EXISTS IN HOW WE LISTEN, NOT HOW WE SPEAK!

Years ago, when Brad was being trained as a coach, he was driving down a freeway in Detroit at high speed. He went to change lanes, but as he did, he heard a loud horn blare and veered back into his own lane. When he looked over his shoulder, he saw a woman driving in the lane alongside, screaming at him. The veins in her forehead were bulging, and she generously shared her middle finger. It's safe to say she was experiencing some road rage.

Brad's initial reaction was to respond in kind. But after thinking about it for a moment, he realized, "She just saved my life. She just pointed out to me that I'm not being careful enough in checking my blind spot." Brad had been coached by that woman...so much so that he still remembers it now, thirty years later. The woman had no intention of being a coach; she only intended to protect herself from an idiot who almost killed her. Brad made a conscious choice to have a growth mindset, listen to her actions, and learn from them. As we say, coaching exists in the way people listen.

Gaining a genuine request for coaching is something you need to discern. Because you are the boss, if you ask people "Are you open to coaching?," almost everyone will say yes, whether they mean it or not. What you need to determine is whether they are genuinely being open or are they just saying yes to comply. Creating a coaching relationship requires caring, openness, and trust.

When we ask people in our programs to define coaching, many say it's the process of asking questions to help another person think through something. Asking questions is a very effective coaching method that's frequently taught, but there are many other ways to coach. Making a suggestion is coaching. Giving someone something to read can be coaching. Almost anything can be coaching if people are listening for coaching.

Most coach-training programs focus on helping people to learn the process of inquiry, or helping people think through a subject through the masterful art of listening and asking questions. This is because most of us stink at asking thought-provoking, open-ended questions that garner insight. Most of us ask closed-ended questions that are fishing for agreement or validation: "Don't you agree?" "Isn't that a great point I just made?" "Do you get great insights from this point?" Those are three examples of the sort of closed-ended questions that most of us ask instead of asking a simple open-ended question such as "What do you think?"

As with leading and managing, it's not a simple matter of adopting new tactics or using new words. Being an effective coach requires generating a very different attitude about other people and how you relate to them. The principal foundation of that mindset is generating an assumption that the person you are coaching is fully capable. We all have judgments and assessments about others: about what they're capable of or what they're not capable of, about whether they're smart or not, whether they're committed or not, or whether they're determined or not. Our Critic naturally looks most closely at their deficits.

To be an effective coach, we actually need to have a mindset that embraces the opposite attitude. You need to assume that the person you are coaching has capabilities that they don't even know they have and that you can't see. Making this leap of faith when you've known someone for some time and they have demon-strated a lack of intelligence or judgment is very difficult. But assuming the best in someone is also very productive.

Think of your favorite teacher, the one who caused you to stretch the most. They were doing exactly what a good coach does: seeing capability, goodness, and even nobility in you that you didn't even see in yourself.

Remember the quote from the great coach Ara Parseghian we referenced earlier: "*A good coach will make his players see what they can be rather than what they are.*"

There are other mindset shifts you need to be a good coach, but they're too involved to get into here; they would require another book! We offer the following practices in the meantime: thegreatengagementbook.com.

PRACTICES FOR EFFECTIVE COACHING

1. Be coachable and ask for coaching. This is often the best way to build a coaching culture. If you are open to coaching, then eventually your team will follow your lead, and they will start asking for coaching as well.

2. Be open to the "perceptions," "perspectives," or "opinions" of others. Be aware that those are their reality.

3. Use The Elevate System™ to develop the Conscious Success Strategies you need to lead, manage, and coach more effectively.

4. Establish a coaching relationship with each member of your team:

    A. Make sure they know you are committed to their success.

    B. Make sure they know it is part of their job to ask for coaching when they encounter barriers.

    C. Provide actionable suggestions to people for the future.

5. Support one another in living all the standards you establish. Offer coaching to your team members...*make sure you have permission first.*

6. Use open-ended questions to help people think through the issues you are coaching them on. This is probably the most useful tool in a coach's repertoire—and not an easy one to use!
7. Reflect on your day. This practice is a great way to become more conscious. What went well? How intentional was your day? What percent of your day was spent leading? What percent of your day was spent managing? What percent of your day was spent coaching? What results did you produce? How could you improve tomorrow?

CHAPTER 15

A DIAGNOSTIC TOOL

"Proper diagnosis is the key to finding the right remedy."

—MAHATMA GANDHI

Leadership, management, and coaching are the three sets of tools necessary to produce results with and through other people. Anytime you face a challenge with an associate, you can use these three as a diagnostic tool. One or more of these three are always missing in someone when there's a performance problem. Paying attention to all three gives you a clue as to what action to take.

- Is the issue that the person just doesn't see the relevance of a project or task? That they don't see how it's connected to what's important to them? Or are they just there for the paycheck and looking to get by with a minimum effort?

Clearly, *leadership* is missing.

- Or are they very committed and inspired but regularly don't deliver what's needed on time? Ask yourself: Did I get a promise? Did I follow up with them before the deadline to remind them? Am I keeping an accounting, a list of what they have promised me so that I can follow up?

In that case, *management* is missing.

- Or are they committed and happy to make a promise, but they don't know how to accomplish what they've promised?

In this case, *coaching* is missing (though the person has to ask for it).

Striving to constantly improve our ability to lead, manage, and coach is a lifetime project. It's also a project that will pay huge rewards: improved relationships, a more meaningful life, greater fulfillment, and accomplishment of your higher purpose.

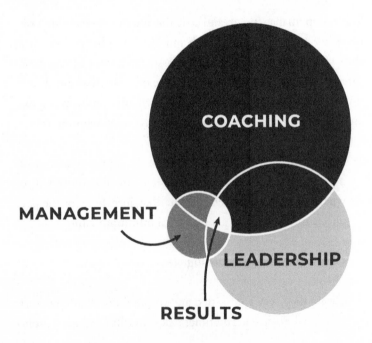

CONCLUSION

Transformational Leadership coupled with Empowering Management and Supportive Coaching works. CEOs who go through a formal process can see growth, both personally and in their organizations. Many continue to benefit without our help, while some employ us to continue to support the transformation throughout the organization.

Either way, transformation never truly ends. Default Success Strategies are powerful drivers of behavior. In times of stress or uncertainty, it's understandable that people retreat to them. Pushing beyond this fear-based space into behavior driven by our higher purpose requires focus, effort, and conscious practices. It's not easy, but here's the good news, which we've seen play out over and over again: *Once an organization declares its higher purpose and focuses on achieving that purpose, it tends to attract employees who have a sense of personal purpose and are dedicated to making a difference.*

Earlier we shared this equation:

Engagement = Aspiration + Empowerment

When leaders go to work on intentionally creating an exceptional culture, they'll notice that all three of these elements act more as a positive, reinforcing cycle.

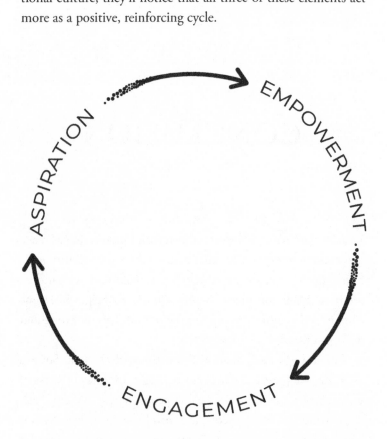

A purpose-driven organization creates a virtuous cycle. The more we practice and reinforce our purpose with one another, the more it becomes part of our culture. In turn, that attracts more people to join. Eventually, the organization reaches critical mass. The majority of team members now understand the power of purpose—and it becomes the dominant way of thinking. When this occurs, it places an organization leagues ahead of counterparts who lack a comparable purpose-driven culture.

FROM RESIGNATION TO ENGAGEMENT

The Great Resignation has created a wake-up call for leaders. It's a call to use every tool they possess to attract and retain top team members. One of the most direct and effective tools is employee engagement.

Most employee engagement efforts address the symptoms of disengagement, not its root cause: resignation. What holds CEOs and organizations back is a failure to understand and work with their conscious purpose. They are limited by their *unconscious* purpose. Leaders seeking to transform their organization must first transform themselves to move past their fear-based Default Success Strategy.

The first step in the transformational process is simply to understand that it exists as a possibility. That's why picking up this book was a crucial first step.

We'd be lying if we said this was easy. You'll need to allow yourself to be real and open (which can feel vulnerable) and ask your team to do the same. That's one of the reasons we recommend using external coaches and facilitators to make the process slightly less uncomfortable.

Culture really does eat everything, so embarking on a cultural transformation process must start at the top when you, as CEO, begin to base your behavior on conscious purpose rather than unconscious strategies; it leads to purpose taking hold throughout the organization, and team members at every level using both their personal purpose and the company purpose to inform their day-to-day decisions. Your purpose starts to impact your work and family life, and those closest to you recognize the positive changes in you. And it stretches out to those interacting with your company, from clients and suppliers to the surrounding community. Most of all, it will bring you engagement and satisfaction you had probably forgotten was even possible from work—driving you on to accomplish more.

We've seen this transformation many times over the past thirty years, yet it never fails to amaze us. It will amaze you, too. It's beautiful to see. People who would have sworn that they are only in it for the paycheck find themselves caring more and working harder once empowered by their true purpose. Organizations proudly declare that they exist not to crank out widgets but to rescue, to empower, to heal, to combat resignation.

DIY OR A PROFESSIONAL APPROACH?

You should understand that while you, as CEO, can lead your team through these exercises, it can be a delicate balancing act. Your position within the organization may make it difficult for you to both facilitate and take part in the process.

Because of this, we recommend that you at least consider hiring a professional. Their guidance will come in handy and will allow you to truly be "a player" with your team, wearing only one hat. If they have coaching skills to assist with any follow-up, so much the better.

If you do go this route, choose your facilitator carefully. Asking tough questions is part of their job; insist that they do so of you, as well as everyone else. Facilitators are human and can be as gun shy as anyone else about putting the CEO on the hot seat, especially if the CEO brought them in—and is signing their paycheck.

If you end up considering a facilitator or a coach, we would be honored if you consider us. Whether you do or not, we suggest that you ensure the following agreements are in place with whomever you choose to hire:

1. They'll be accountable for results, not just for working through a process.
2. They'll be a true partner who cares deeply about *your* success.

3. They'll have a very specific and methodical approach to helping your team operate in new ways while at the same time helping individuals change their behavior. They'll deliver a team process and an individual process in parallel.

4. They'll help you develop a "coaching culture" where each of you will support one another in the behavioral development that you committed to. Without this support, people are left on their own, and the change effort will collapse.

5. They'll help you develop a sustainable structure to help ensure that this process cascades down through the organization.

6. They'll use a multidisciplinary approach. For example, our approach combines breakthrough workshops with individual coaching; team coaching; a CEO roundtable for presidents, CEOs, and school superintendents from across the country; a series of weekly videos to remind people of concepts and spur them into action; and our coaching tool, the Elevate System, to give people insight they can use for coaching each other.

7. They'll be able to give you references, such as past clients who can attest not only to the transformation that took place in their organization but how that transformation resulted in measurable results such as customer satisfaction, employee retention, and profitability.

One word of caution: As a CEO who embarks on this adventure, whether you use a facilitator or do it on your own, you need to be prepared to face normal human reactions and must also master your own emotional responses and reactions—especially *defensiveness.*

Defensive responses among participants are extremely common:

"Impatient? You bet I am! Have you seen my workload lately?"

If you're using a professional facilitator, it's *their* job to head off problems like this and ensure that participants truly hear the feedback and coaching they're being offered. If you are acting as facilitator, it's *your* job…and you have to be doubly on your guard not to be defensive yourself.

Sometimes the person having trouble absorbing feedback is *you*.

INFINITE LOVE

Earlier, we shared that at the heart of transformational leadership is what the Greeks called agape love: a willful, sacrificial love that takes delight in working for the growth or benefit of others. In the words of Roman Catholic philosopher Peter Kreeft, "This is the secret of life: the self lives only by dying, finds its identity (and its happiness) only by self-forgetfulness, self-giving, self-sacrifice, and agape love."

Transformation and agape love are an infinite game. There is no "there" to get to; there is only somewhere a little further along the path—and the path of improving ourselves by helping others never ends. Human software is like computer software: it needs to be updated regularly. When we stop updating our software, we stop growing. We become resigned, and obsolescence quickly sets in.

Exceptional leaders don't allow this to persist. They create exceptional cultures by understanding that true transformation is an iterative process, and they are always pursuing the best version of themselves and the best version of each and every one of those they are entrusted and blessed to lead.

So forget all about the Great Resignation. It's time for the Great Engagement. It's time to change the world. It's time for transformation.

"BASICALLY, WHEN YOU GET TO MY
AGE, YOU'LL REALLY MEASURE YOUR
SUCCESS IN LIFE BY HOW MANY OF
THE PEOPLE YOU WANT TO HAVE
LOVE YOU ACTUALLY DO LOVE YOU."

—WARREN BUFFETT

ACKNOWLEDGMENTS

BRAD ZIMMERMAN

This book is a compilation of what I've learned over my career and what I've tried to convey to clients. You could say it's my life's work on paper. So I'd like to thank the following people for their contribution to the work and to my life: I've listed them in chronological order.

To my father, Hal Zimmerman: you taught me the value of hard work and integrity, and helped me start my first business when I was twelve. For those lessons, I will be forever in your debt.

To my wife Gwen: you have faith in me when I have no faith in myself, over and over and over again in my life.

To my dad again: when I went to him in late 1990 and told him I was going to sell the family business and become a coach, I was sure he was going to be angry. After all, the business was his baby as much as I was. To my surprise, all he said was "How can I help?"

To Jon Greenwald, my coach and business partner: you had major reservations about whether I could be successful as a coach, but took me on as a partner anyway. Without your help, I never could have had this great career.

To Mark Stein, another business partner: for twenty-one years, we experimented together to create what is now this body of work, producing surprising transformations with thousands of clients.

To 10,000 clients: I thank them for their willingness to take the risk of trusting that I could help them grow. There are a number of those I've worked with for over a decade whose confidence, especially during times of self-doubt, empowered me to keep going—you know who you are.

And lastly, to Tom Willis: without you encouraging me, pushing me to commit to writing this book with you, it would never have been written. Thank you for making this work new again.

TOM WILLIS

Brad, thank you. It's a blessing to have you as a business partner, friend, and coach. You've forever transformed the trajectory of my life.

Jessica, I fall more in love with you every day. It's like magic being married to you.

Anna, Molly & Peter, you continue to teach me about the things that matter. I will love you forever. And ever.

Dad, I miss you beyond words. If all this book does is make you smile, it will have exceeded my expectations.

Mom, you taught me what love is truly all about.

Brothers, you've always been my heroes (even though you're just learning of that now).

Delaney, Cole, Luke, Jenn, Julie, Matthew, Lynn & Brad, you are blessings. Thank you for loving on me in your awesomely unique ways.

God, You are Love. Help me as I continue to try to listen and be closer to You every day.

ABOUT THE
AUTHORS

BRAD ZIMMERMAN believes there is unlimited potential in the human spirit, and that we all adopt beliefs that can limit our potential, but that we can regain access to this potential to unleash personal and organizational growth. Brad is one of the most experienced business coaches in the country—he started in 1991, and has worked with more than 10,000 clients. In his spare time, Brad enjoys time with his wife of forty-one years, their kids, and their six grandkids. He is a member of the Board of Trustees of The Judson Center, a provider of children's services, and an active fundraiser for Make-A-Wish.

TOM WILLIS, at age thirty-four, became a CEO of an innovative and inspirational school system in Detroit. He loves helping CEOs, presidents, school superintendents, and other leaders become the best versions of themselves. As a former classroom teacher, he believes in the power of lifelong learning. His primary goal in life is helping others move beyond their self-limiting beliefs so they can reach their potential. He was fortunate to earn an engineering degree from the University of Michigan and an MBA from the University of Notre Dame. He is also an International Coach Federation (ICF) certified coach. Tom thanks God every day for his amazing wife and three wonderful children.

Together, Tom and Brad have tens of thousands of hours of training, executive coaching, and workshop leadership. They've helped organizations from Kenai, Alaska, to Stuttgart, Germany, with their proven method to help people transform how they see themselves, their team members, and their purpose in the world.

Brad, Tom, and the entire Phoenix Performance Partners team believe deeply that Culture is the most powerful tool any organization has, and thus they're working hard to create a world-wide movement that helps every leader understand that *Culture Eats Everything!* Every team member considers themselves a cultural catalyst, and they are on a mission to transform the world by helping others transform their cultures. They provide CEOs with a Catalyst that changes their cultural ecosystem. This catalyst results in a chain reaction, starting with a profound growth for the individuals and then a shift in the social dynamics of the team, which generates exceptional business results. And their unique combination of extraordinary team members and their proprietary system makes it possible for them to promise dramatic changes in the cultural ecosystem for every client.

Made in the USA
Las Vegas, NV
29 January 2024

85068838R00132